CREATING GOOD
LANDSCAPE DESIGN
A GUIDE FOR NON-PROFESSIONALS

By Glen Hunt & Eugene Smith

226 Second Avenue West, Seattle, WA 98119 • 206-281-5965

Library of Congress No. 95-067927
Hunt, Glen and Smith, Eugene
Creating Good Landscape Design
ISBN 0-89716-561-6
11.0025
Cover design by Robert Dietz
Production: Elizabeth Lake

First printing February 1995
10 9 8 7 6 5 4 3 2 1

Peanut Butter Publishing
226 2nd Avenue West
Seattle, WA 98119

Printed in the United States of America

Table of Contents

Dedicated to the memory of Glen Hunt.
This book had been his dream.
He lived to see the manuscript completed,
but not the printing and distribution.
He would have been delighted to see his dream realized.

Looking for a way to professionally design your own landscape? Here's the book that will enable your to create you own plan. The late Glen Hunt and his friend Eugene Smith have combined talents to make it possible for homeowners to step-by-step plan and design the garden and landscape of their dreams.

Ed Hume
Gardening Expert

GLEN HUNT REMEMBERED

written by Elizabeth Rivers
President-elect of the Washington Chapter
American Society of Landscape Architects
January 1995

Glen Hunt, FASLA, was a landscape architect, plantsman, activist, teacher, author, father and grandfather, brother and uncle, and friend to many. Glen died in Seattle on October 26, 1994, at age 73 of leukemia.

Glen was a completely open person, who nevertheless remained somewhat of an enigma. Considering the breadth and depth of his involvement in his profession, in his community and with his family and friends, the air of mystery about him may have simply been from not being able to keep up with him. Of the many facets of Glen's life and personality he was, above all, a landscape architect. His earliest experience was focused on plants and he built on that interest to develop an expertise that combined extensive knowledge of plants with a strong sense of design.

Glen was a native of Seattle whose formal education was interrupted by his service in the Army Air Corps during World War II. Prior to that, he studied botany and horticulture, but influenced by army leave spent touring gardens in England, he returned to Washington State University and, in 1951, graduated in landscape architecture. He opened an office in North Seattle on March 27, 1954, which evolved into Glen Hunt and Associates. His Washington State license in landscape architecture, number 53, reflects his long career. He worked with, and learned from, noted early area landscape architects Otto Holmdahl and John Grant.

Glen's extensive work throughout the Northwest includes parks, institutional, commercial, and residential projects. Many of Glen's projects have been recognized and awarded by both the American Institute of Landscape Architects, American Society of Landscape Architects, Master Builders, and other professional organizations.

He was affiliated with the American Institute of Landscape Architects and served as national president of that organization in 1975-76. He joined the American Society of Landscape Architects in 1970, and was an active member of ASLA on both the state and national level. He received the Washington Chapter ASLA Award for Distinguished Service in 1980. He chaired the ASLA Open Committee for Residential Landscape Architecture from 1988 to 1990. In 1982, Glen was recognized for his many contributions to the profession and this organization by his election to the ASLA College of Fellows.

Friends and family remember him as a teacher who shared his knowledge unreservedly. Glen's lifelong interest in education was manifested in many ways. In addition to teaching at the University of Washington and in community colleges throughout the state, Glen furthered public interest in residential landscape architecture and plants through his retail nursery teaching program. Glen was an Honorary Lifetime Member of the Washington State Nursery and Landscape Association and chaired the WSNLA's Education Committee.

He served on the WSNLA Board of Directors and was President of the Seattle Chapter of the WSNLA from 1992 to 1994. Last year, the WSNLA recognized Glen's contribution to their organization and to the nursery industry by presenting him with their highest honor, the Outstanding Service Award. Glen participated in many other organizations that further understanding and appreciation of plants and gardens. He was a member of the University of Washington Arboretum Foundation and a Board Member of the Seattle Chinese Garden Society. Far beyond counting were the number of garden tours and field trips he organized and led.

Glen remained an active outdoorsman throughout his life (hiking Tiger Mountain at age 72) and was an early member of the Mountaineers. This interest provided a foundation for his use of native plants in his work.

Glen recognized that care of the environment went far beyond the traditional scope of landscape architecture. He was a member of the Washington State Arts Commission from 1975 to 1979 and in 1989, chair of the Washington State Centennial Committee. He contributed time and energy to study the causes of, and ways of reducing, vandalism in public areas. His work through the Washington State Roadside Council focused on elimination of billboards, screening of parking and roadways, and parkway landscaping.

In 1970, with a group of engineers, architects and planners, Glen helped form Environmental Professionals Northwest. The coalition added environmental scientists and researchers onto the team in an early attempt to address the wider ecological needs of environmental design. Glen's explanation of their goal remains valid twenty-five years later, "We plan as a group to pursue site investigations, soil and water studies, stream control, plant and tree studies, wildlife studies (with recommendations to not only save birds and animals, but to have animal communities)."

Glen's contribution to understanding and appreciation of the designed and natural environment extended to published articles. His written articles and articles featuring his work were published in *Architecture West*, *Better Homes & Gardens*, and *Sunset* magazines and in numerous newspapers throughout the Northwest. Last year he completed a ten-year writing project that resulted in Glen's final teaching effort, the publication of this book.

The landscape architects and designers at Glen Hunt and Associates were privileged to be in the position to learn from Glen firsthand every day. The firm continues to implement his philosophies and principles of design in their work.

ACKNOWLEDGMENTS

Landscape architects:
     Bob Heins, Port Orchard WA
     Elizabeth Rivers, ASLA, Seattle WA
     Charles Steele, ASLA, Bloomington IN

Members of American Society of Landscape Architects:
     Bill Butler, FL
     Al David, Dallas TX
     Hal Gausman, Custer SD
     Barbara Jones, Redwood City CA
     Wesley Lent, Woodbury CT
     Jerry Lewis, El Paso TX
     Roy Pender, Danbury CT
     Joan Radditz, Santa Barbara CA
     David Racker, Bountiful UT
     Gerald Rewolinski, WI
     Robert Wakeland, FL

Member of Canadian Society of Landscape Architects:
     R. Hugh Knowles, Edmonton AB, Canada

Graphic artists:
     Bob Hart
     Ray Higa
     Madeline Partridge
     Mark Webster
     Dr. John Wott

Staff members of Glen Hunt Associates:
     Neil Buchanan
     Fauna Gibson
     Kevin Hunt
     Mark Webster

Library staff at Center for Urban Horticulture, University of Washington:
     Valerie Easton
     Martha Ferguson
     Elisabeth C. Miller
     Laura Lipton

TO OUR READERS

Perhaps this is the first time you have turned your attention seriously to landscaping a house or other building. If so, you may have thought that all you needed was a big enough budget to buy several plants and trees of various kinds so you could stick them in wherever there is space. After all, plantings around a building look better to almost everybody than bare ground or weeds.

But perhaps you are farther along in your thinking about the art of landscaping. You may realize that there's more to a successful job of landscaping than just choosing the right plants for your climate and digging holes wherever there's space. You probably have an inkling that good landscaping happens only when the landscaper has a good design.

How do you get a good design? Certainly not by just going outside and eyeballing the place ("A pine might be good there," "Why not put some yews as a border by the sidewalk?" "I'd like to see a few evergreens and maybe some flowering plants for color").

We hope you'll have little trouble agreeing with us that novice landscapers need help at two main stages of landscaping:

1) creating the landscape design
2) carrying out the design

Providing that help is what this book is all about. It shows you how a professional landscape architect thinks about landscaping—from abstract principles of balance and beauty to preparing the site properly—and it guides you as you learn to think and act like a designer. As in most other human activities, you'll become more comfortable with that way of thinking as you train your eyes and use your hands to carry out the design.

Whether you are a student in a high school or college landscaping course or an individual who wants to landscape his or her own home, you'll find in this book all you need to know about creating beautiful physical surroundings. We think your spirit will benefit, too.

INTRODUCTION

A good way for you to begin thinking about landscape design is to listen to people who really know the subject. Having conversations with landscape architects, professional or even amateur gardeners, and teachers of landscape design courses would be ideal.

But it's not always easy to find such people when you need them. Instead, we can help you "overhear" excerpts from conversations:

A garden should fit the owner's personality. After all, the designer, unless it's the owner him- or herself, is not going to live there. But I also believe gardens are as important as the buildings they accompany. They are architecture just as buildings are—that is, a series of planned spaces.

* * *

Well-planned gardens are individuals; no two gardens are alike. Gardens should express the owner's personality and how she wants to use the space. But there are certain rules or methods of design to follow if the garden is worthy of being judged. The house should be an integral part of a landscape design. Ask yourself, as you judge a design, questions like these:

> **Are there pleasing relationships between the house and the property, such as forms, shapes, walks, patios, decks, etc.?**
>
> **Do the house and garden spaces flow together in design, color, and materials?**
>
> **Is the style of the home expressed in the landscape somehow?**
>
> **Has the house been situated to make the best use of the land—the views, the soils and drainage, and the climatic conditions?**
>
> **Do the inside spaces or rooms extend, wherever possible, into the outdoor areas?**
>
> **Have parts of the garden become useful total microclimates— with both sunny and shady areas, out of the way of cold winds and drifting snows?**

* * *

Gardens are composed of many elements and materials. The organization of all parts of a garden should make one composition, including the house. The garden must have a sense of unity. When you look at the garden, you pay attention to how the patterns, the colors, and the masses created by plants and any other materials fit together overall. It's like pretending to look at the whole thing from a great distance—the way astronauts perceive the earth from their crafts. Details recede in prominence and relationships become easier to see. That's how to learn to discern unity. Without unity, the garden has no composition, no character, and no assurance of being a real enhancement to living on that site.

* * *

Plants play a very important part in people's lives, even though people aren't always conscious of the effects on them of plants they see every day. Whether I'm in Indiana or Arizona or Maine or Oregon, I explore the parks, looking especially for the native plants. I try to take a lesson from Nature in each of these regions, because Nature has distributed plants to suit the conditions. Gardeners had better work with Nature if they want long-lasting and satisfying results. They'll save money, too, if they design their gardens around plants that are known to grow well in that climate. Beware the exotic!

* * *

Anybody who tends plants for a living sees that native plants are always the best choice for looks and for all-season maintenance. I favor xeriscapes. They're arrangements of plants that take almost no water—no more, anyway, than Nature regularly supplies in the form of rain. You can't beat a xeriscape for low maintenance, and if you get the combination of plants right, you'd be surprised how appealing it is to the eye. It doesn't have to be six varieties of cactus either!

* * *

What is the mood of the garden I am judging? Does it excite, stimulate, or relax people using the garden spaces? Gardens have personalities. Some gardens have a certain aura that holds my interest, makes me want to return to them. They aren't all natural types, either. Sometimes I like to see roses in bloom at the formal garden in the city park.

* * *

Do the outdoor spaces—such as, patios, decks, garden work spaces, vegetable gardens, recreation spaces for both adults and children, and especially the connecting walkway system—relate to one another? In other words, are they all parts of a unified composition?

* * *

    I do like to see good workmanship in carrying out the design: the right material for function. For instance, if the patio is to be used for dancing, it should be smooth. If we're going to move tables and chairs over a patio, let's not pave the area in cobblestones or plant moss between the pavers.

* * *

    What about the objects within these special spaces? For instance, a quiet sitting area, a reflection pool or sundial, steps, a planter: are they also an integral part of the space, not just an afterthought plunked into a design that they'll never suit? Are these objects useful and tasteful? (Do we really need pink plastic flamingos?) Do they relate to the people using these objects?

    If you were to boil these excerpts down to principles or general statements about how landscape designers think, you might come up with the following:

- Beauty is not, as the cliché goes, in the eye of the beholder. Beauty is the result of applying certain principles of design.
- Harmony is important in design: bringing all the elements together into a unified whole.
- Each home owner should have the type of landscape—building materials, plants, and special objects of interest—that she wants, to suit that owner's personality.

    You need to know, too, that as a result of following these principles carefully, home owners protect and even add to the value (20 to 50% by many estimates) of the biggest investment they ever make—their homes. If they will take the time to make a design, even before they touch a trowel or move a rock, they will have a direction for the coming years of home occupancy. They'll save many hours of retracing or redoing areas in the landscape, and they'll budget their money for best use over several years.

    The well-designed landscape can be the blueprint to the future.

Chapter 1

THE DESIGN PROCESS

The voices you overheard in the introduction may have focused your attention on the indispensable need for a design. In the wild, Nature creates arrays of plants and rocks that are inherently appealing, but when humans intervene we must consciously design; attractive gardens don't just happen by random or haphazard combining of elements.

The design process doesn't have to be complicated, but it requires enthusiasm, creativity, and a mind open to possibilities. It occurs best when such objections as the following are overruled or suppressed:

Objection: Making a design costs too much. There are more important places
to spend money.

Reply: NO, A GOOD DESIGN ISN'T EXPENSIVE IN RELATION TO THE
REST OF THE LANDSCAPING PROJECT. IN FACT, A GOOD DESIGN
CAN SAVE YOU MONEY BY HELPING YOU AVOID COSTLY MISTAKES.

Objection: Who cares about the outdoor areas? The inside of the house is
where we spend our time.

Reply: BUT MOST PEOPLE ADD MUCH PLEASURE TO THEIR LIVES
BY SPENDING A GOOD DEAL OF TIME OUTSIDE, DON'T THEY?
TALKING WITH FRIENDS; EATING BREAKFAST, LUNCH, OR SUPPER;
READING AND LISTENING TO MUSIC; OR JUST ABSORBING THE
CALMING AND STEADYING INFLUENCE OF NATURAL THINGS:
ALL THESE ACTIVITIES ARE ENHANCED BY DOING THEM IN
ATTRACTIVE SURROUNDINGS THAT EXTEND THE INSIDE
LIVING SPACE.

Objection: I don't want a garden. They're too much work. I don't like to mow
lawns, weed flower beds, tend plants.

Reply: FINE. YOU CAN DESIGN AN ATTRACTIVE OUTDOOR SPACE
THAT DOESN'T REQUIRE ANY OF THESE HIGH-MAINTENANCE
TASKS.

Objection: I'd rather watch TV, tinker with the car, go on camping trips.
Reply: WELL, IN THAT CASE, MAYBE YOU SHOULD LIVE IN A CONDO AND LET SOMEBODY ELSE THINK ABOUT LANDSCAPING!

If the idea of attractive outdoor living spaces does appeal to you—as it does to most people—you can learn how to make a design relatively easily. As you become familiar with design principles, the property or land you want to make fit for certain uses or functions will take shape in your mind—gradually and with organization.

While you may not consciously adhere to definite phases in your effort to get a design, many people who have gone through the design process recognize stages that might be labelled as follows:

Inspiration: A germ of what might be settles into the mind. Maybe a fresh coat of paint has renewed an awareness that paint on the house exterior isn't quite enough to make it look right. Or perhaps we look around at neighbors' houses and see that some of these folks have acted on a bright idea and created an eye-catching effect with a landscape design. We think, "Well, I wouldn't have done it quite that way, but . . ." That's enough to get the inspirational juices flowing.

Imagination: Once the germ has taken hold, it probably won't go away quickly or easily. It'll lie there, affecting you each time you look at your house or any space that you might have some control over. Then, as you gather more ideas by further observations, visits to nurseries, perhaps some leafing through of books about landscaping, your imagination is being fed—adding to your options and opening possibilities that you weren't even aware of before.

Organization: Just as putting up a durable building is unthinkable without a written and highly organized plan, so a landscape design must have careful organization. Shapes, sizes, and textures all need to be coherently put together.

Here's a checklist of things for any prospective landscape designer to do very early in the process:

- Getting acquainted with the site: carefully observing soils, drainage, exposure to the elements, views of both appealing and unappealing vistas, existing features (including plants and trees, neighbors, rocks, slope of the land).
- Getting acquainted with the house: its relationship to outdoor spaces on all sides, doors and windows (including desirable and undesirable views from inside), house style and materials.
- Listing your requirements: your needs and desires about entries (by foot and by car or other vehicle), parking space, walkways, decking, open space, quiet spaces. Think about present and future requirements.

If you'll start making both mental and written notes to yourself about the items on this checklist, you are well on the way to creating your landscape design. In the next chapter, we look at how you can move from early inspiration and imagination phases to organization and execution—without, of course, suggesting that inspiration and imagination won't be your steady companions through the whole landscaping process.

Chapter 2

ASSESSING YOUR REQUIREMENTS FOR A GARDEN

Your garden, or the garden you are about to design, will be different from every other existing garden because it will fit your specific requirements. If it doesn't, you'll long regret not having designed it to suit your needs and desires. That's why we urge you to list them in detail. Thinking vaguely about what your garden should be will probably result in a botched job.

To help you do detailed thinking about your (and your family's) garden requirements, we present a series of worksheets, with our questions and reminders on the left and space for you to note the specifics of these requirements on the right. We are, in other words, urging you to produce a well-developed inventory of specifications.

PEOPLE REQUIREMENTS

If your garden is to be a place for continuing enjoyment and relaxation for the whole family, every family member should have a role in garden planning. They should all answer this question: How do we want to use our garden?

Who will use the garden?

Adults:

_____

_____

For what purposes?

_____

_____

_____

Children:

_____

_____

All parts of the design must be suitable to the people who use the property.

For what purposes?

_____

_____

_____

Consider uses such as these:

— entertaining (type & frequency; desired areas, such as decks, other hard surfaces, patio, hot tub; average amount of time each year that your climate permits outdoor living)

_____

_____

— animals (both domesticated and wild) and whether they will be invited into the garden

_____

— hobbies (e.g., model railroading, wheeled vehicles, sports—from croquet to swimming)

_____

— children's play (noting especially the possible need to shield children from busy streets or other hazards)

_____

_____

STREETSIDE REQUIREMENTS

When friends arrive, where will they park their cars, motorcycles, bicycles, skateboards? Will they be able to turn around or back out of the alley or driveway easily and safely? Will other traffic be able to get by?

Providing for friends' arriving:

parking:_____

_____

_____

maneuvering:_____

_____

_____

What sort of walkway system to your front and back doors do you want? How can it seem inviting and safe?

Walkway(s) from arrival place to house:

_____

_____

_____

_____

_____

What type and amount of privacy from passers-by on the street will you need? Will you want an entry courtyard that can be used as an alternate sitting or eating area? Will you need fencing or plantings that screen activity from outside view?

Privacy requirements:

_____

_____

_____

_____

SERVICE AREAS

What equipment that you have or anticipate having will need storage (e.g., trailers, boats, major tools)?

Large equipment storage areas:

_____

_____

_____

Will you be stacking wood for fireplace or stove? How much at any one time (allowing for adequate seasoning of wood before burning)?

Areas to stack cut firewood:

_____

_____

_____

Will you have a clothes drying area with clothesline?

Area for drying clothes:

_____

_____

Do you need a dog run?

Dog exercise area:

_____

_____

5

What garden work space is desirable: small greenhouse? heated seeding and cutting beds? place for small tools, flower pots, etc.?

Work space for gardening tasks and storage:

_____

_____

_____

Would you like an area to grow vegetables and/or berries? fruit trees?

Area for growing small vegetables and fruit:

_____

_____

_____

Where will you place packaged household trash and recyclables (paper, glass, and some plastics)?

Household trash and recycling storage areas:

_____

_____

_____

How about a compost area? (We all have to compost, whenever we can, but you may not need a large area.)

Compost area:

_____

_____

_____

ENCLOSING ELEMENTS

Although you may know at this point only approximately where you may want fencing and screening, and you may not fully anticipate the relationship of possible future buildings (such as, bedroom addition or remodeling of kitchen) to the garden, you may recognize certain preferences for enclosing elements.

Fence(s) to shield what from what?

_____

_____

_____

_____

Register here some of your current preferences:
    fencing (wood, metal)
    trellises (wood, wire)
    hedges
    screening trees

Other screening:

_____

_____

_____

Chapter 3

DESIGNING GARDEN SPACES: SOME NECESSARY PRELIMINARIES

If you have followed our suggestion for listing your specific needs, you may now feel ready to figure out how to create a garden space that meets those needs. In other words, you are, we hope, in a high state of readiness to learn how to make your own design. Remember: we are stressing that you will most likely be unhappy with any actual landscaping you do unless you're working from a good design in the first place.

Maybe the notion that you yourself can actually create a "good design" scares you a little. Do you, like so many adults, consider yourself no artist? "Can't even draw a straight line"? "Never was any good at sketching"? If so, try not to believe that inner voice that says you can't do it. We'll show you how.

Everyone is quite capable of designing garden spaces. You don't have to be an artist. You do have to acquire a technique for transforming the specific requirements you listed in the previous chapter to specific shapes in the landscape. We'll be working on a series of shapes that will eventually result in a composition—that is, a design. You'll be getting the feeling of how shapes and patterns flow together.

So, get a few soft pencils or a felt-tip pen—whatever kind of drawing instrument feels comfortable and unintimidating to you. Maybe you'll even want to start with a piece of colored chalk to draw on a big piece of newsprint or on a concrete floor. (You can scale back to smaller sheets of paper later, after you get over the initial feeling of tightness about "sketching.") If you'd like to bring other family members in as soon as possible on creating your landscape design, this might be a good time to put pencil, pen, or chalk in their hands, too. Let them have at it along with you—over soft drinks and popcorn or whatever else is going to free you from inhibition. (You ought to be showing your design ideas to others pretty soon anyway, so why not let them share the fun right from the beginning?) Hold the pen or pencil as you would a paintbrush, not the way you would hold it to write.

Now for a little surprise. We're not going to tell you to even draw the shape of your house on the paper or floor. If it's perfectly square, drawing your house shape is no big deal, but maybe your house has a few squiggles and therefore might be hard to draw with any accuracy.

Instead, let's just start with lines of various kinds. Some horizontal ones, like these:

Fig. 3.1

And some diagonal ones:

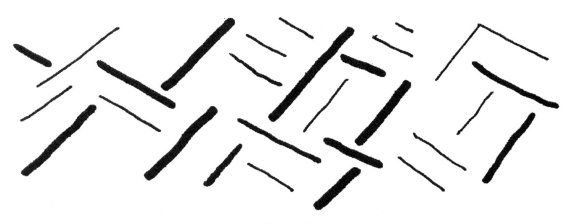

Fig. 3.2

A couple of bent lines:

Fig. 3.3

Straight lines that form a group but don't intersect:

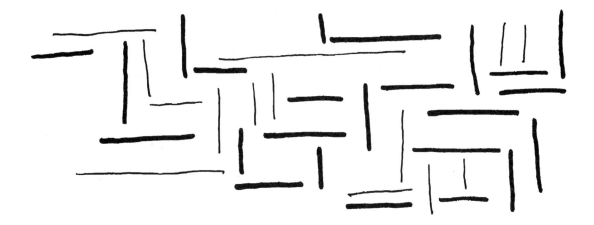

Fig. 3.4

Now try lines of various thickness or density. Thin and delicate lines:

Fig. 3.5

Heavy, dynamic lines (that is, lines that seem to have energy or power):

Fig. 3.6

And a combination of thin and dynamic:

Fig. 3.7

Next, draw a continuous line that moves at angles (or you could think of this as a series of connected lines):

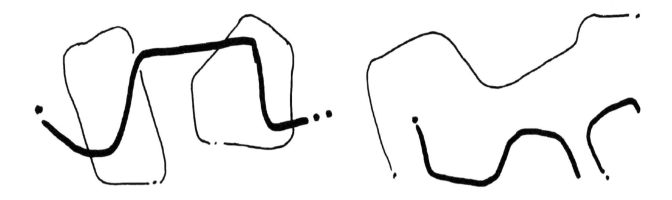

Fig. 3.8

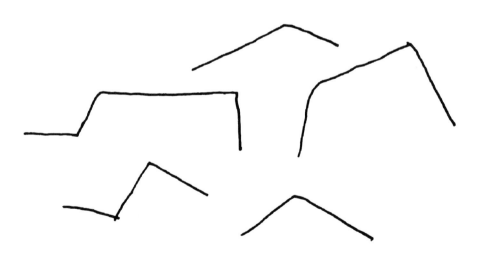

Fig. 3.9

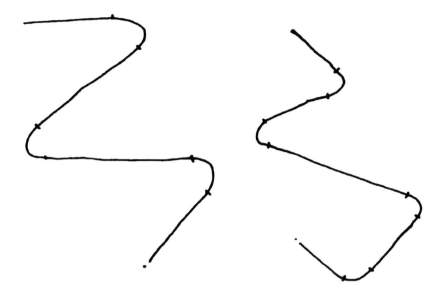

Fig. 3.10

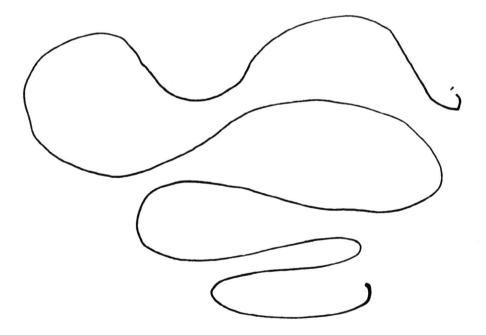

Fig. 3.11

O.K. Brace yourself. Now you should move toward drawing something that will look like a shape—you know, the beginnings of drawing a house shape or a tree shape or a plant container shape. Shapes can start moulding spaces—and it's spaces you're going to be dealing with. Just draw a few connected straight lines and then move into a curve or two, an angle and another angle or curve. (Curves are lines, of course. We don't want you to think that your landscape design will consist only of straight lines and sharp angles. You will want things to flow together, won't you?)

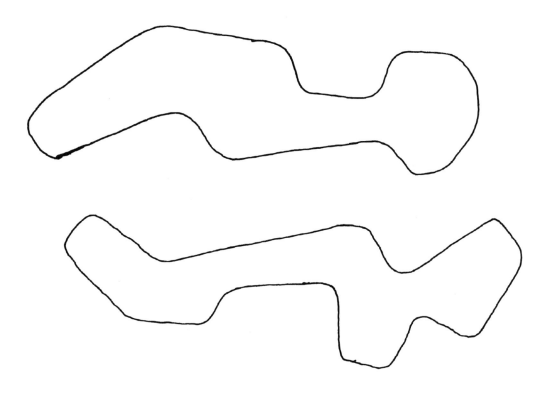

Fig. 3.12

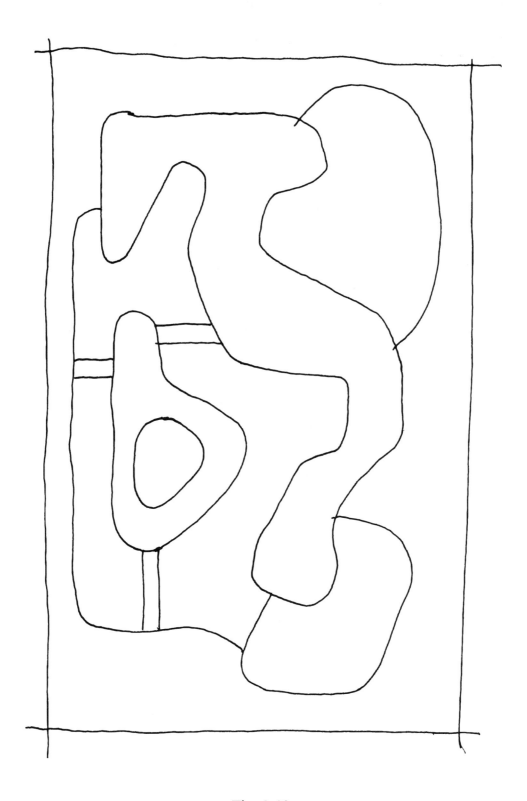

Fig. 3.13

Maybe you can start to see how these straight and curved lines you are drawing are going to represent walkways, garden beds, and other elements in your own landscape design.

Next activity: draw groups of lines like the following that are going to take on a three-dimensional quality. Decks and lawns, for instance, may need to be shown three-dimensionally in your design.

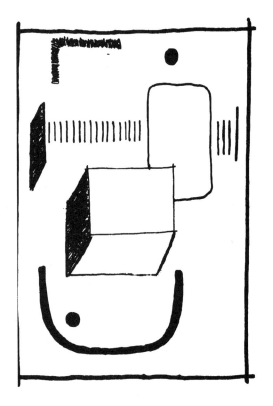 

Fig. 3.14

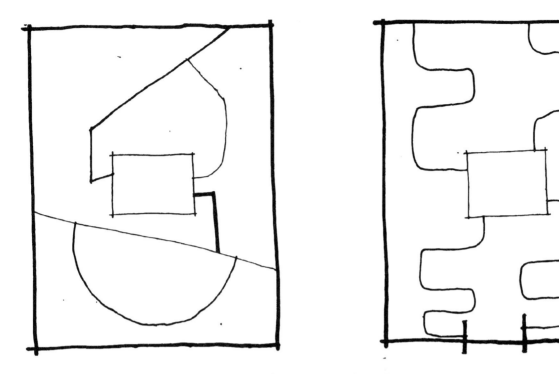

Fig. 3.14 continued

Put some of these preliminaries of sketching into a simple figure. Draw a rectangle and put a shape inside it. Relate your shape to the sides; that is, make the shape somehow visually connected to the containing rectangle. Give the shape variety. Stop and look at the shape and then consider adding some little feature to give it greater interest, but cease when it starts looking too busy (that is, confusingly full of lines and shapes). Here's the beginning of one possible way to do this exercise, but don't just copy this one (yours will be larger):

Fig. 3.15

Do several of these shapes-within-rectangles sketches, each different. After you've made several, you should start getting the feel of a "composition." There will be a point at which you realize you're not just drawing random lines; instead, your hand and eye are leading you to find and execute arrangements of lines and shapes that are organized in some loose way.

Lay the several sketches—compositions—you've made out on a table so you can look at all of them together. You're now going to apply some analysis to your spontaneous creations.

Maybe you'd agree that the sketch below has become too busy, overdone to the point that it has lost any identity or obvious visual appeal:

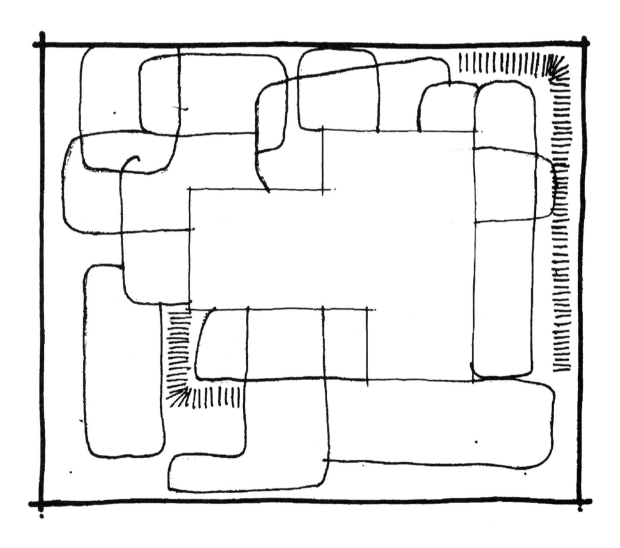

Fig. 3.16

Concluding that a design has lost its identity raises a question about how we arrive at that judgment. What implicit principles or guidelines may we be using to draw a negative judgment about a particular design? We suggest the most important principle or criterion is unity: the feeling that everything in a composition or group fits together. But that's a pretty vague criterion. Isn't one person's notion of unity different from another's? Maybe so.

Professional designers, though, do pretty much agree on when a composition has unity and when it does not. They do it by subdividing the concept of unity into smaller elements: repetition, sequence, variety, balance, harmony, and scale and proportion. As we explain and illustrate each of these elements, cast your eye occasionally at your sketches and note where you have, perhaps subconsciously, included them in your drawing.

Repetition. Most humans seem to find a certain amount of repetition satisfying. Too much repetition equals monotony, though, so we have to find the dividing line. In a landscape design, we can repeat several kinds of features:

- size and form, as in shrubs and paving stones:

Fig. 3.17

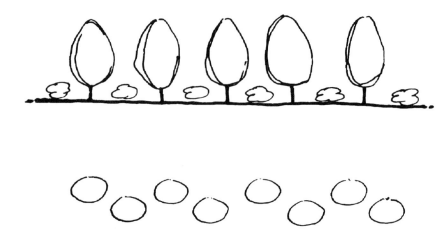

Fig. 3.17 continued

- textures, as in paving materials and types of plant foliage:

Fig. 3.18

• shapes, as in plant varieties, fences, or flowers:

Fig. 3.19

Sequence. Different sequences or arrangements of objects create different rhythms. Just as a 1-2-3 beat, with the heaviest emphasis on 1, defines a waltz rhythm, so we can create a rhythm with visual shapes. We can have a sequence of continuation like this (an almost literal repetition):

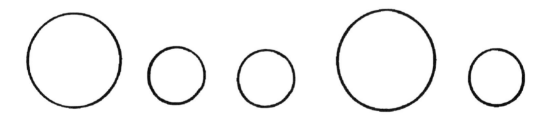

Fig. 3.20

- or a sequence of alternation, repeating two shapes:

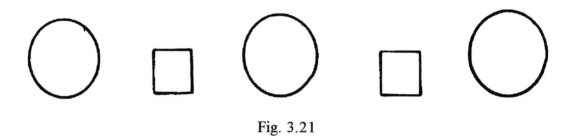

Fig. 3.21

- or a sequence of progression:

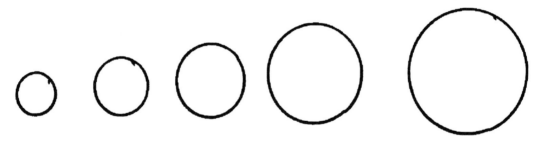

Fig. 3.22

Notice the orderly change from one form to another, a forcing of the eye to perceive unity.

Variety. Just at the point that repetition and sequence threaten to create boredom, we can introduce variety to revive interest in the repeated pattern. Contrast is the lever here, as in these two pairs of shapes, one using plant material, the other harder surfaces:

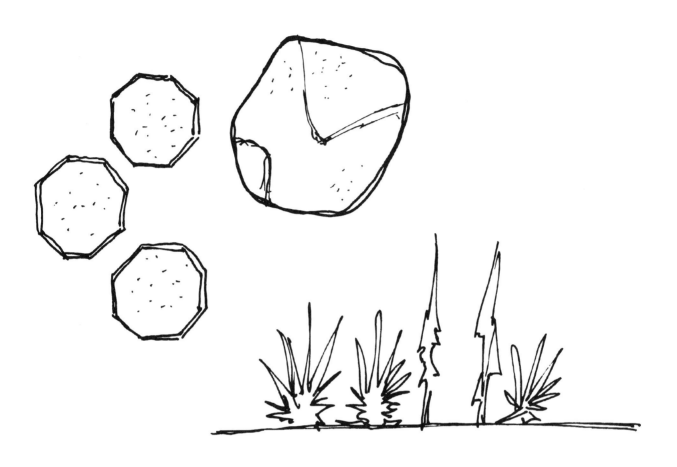

Fig. 3.23

Balance. A possibly inherent human desire in design is for balance: we like to have related objects situated according to some discernible scheme of equilibrium. That can be accomplished both through symmetry and asymmetry. Following are two types of symmetrical balance:

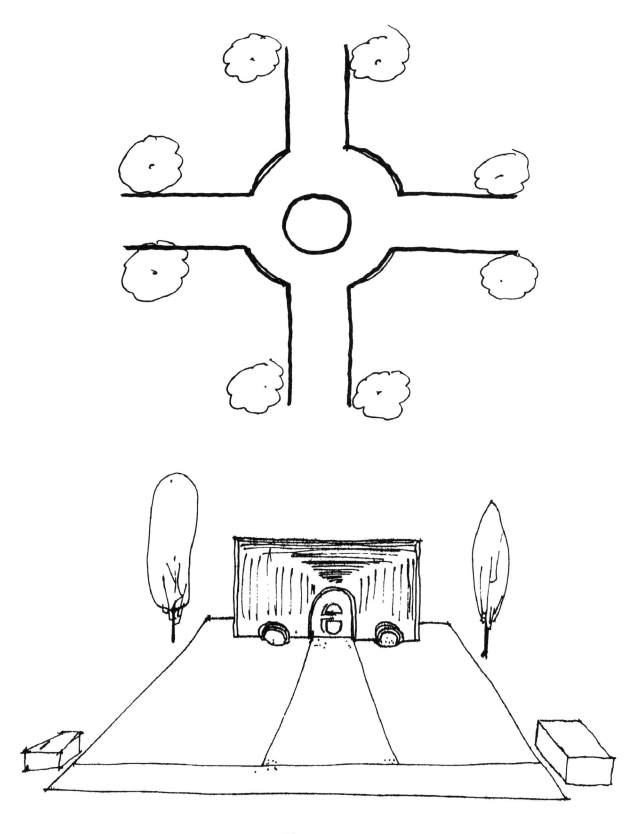

Fig. 3.24

Here are examples of <u>asymmetrical</u> balance, which can be tied to landscape design through choices of mass or overall shape, texture of plant and non-living materials, color, and special interest objects (such as, statuary or fountain):

Fig. 3.25

Figure 3.25 continued

Harmony. Harmony in music is achieved by using traditional chord structures, for example. In visual designs, we sense lack of harmony when objects strike us as disproportional or discordant, just as a musical instrument that is out of tune can skew a chord and create dissonance. See if you agree that these pairs of shapes lack harmony:

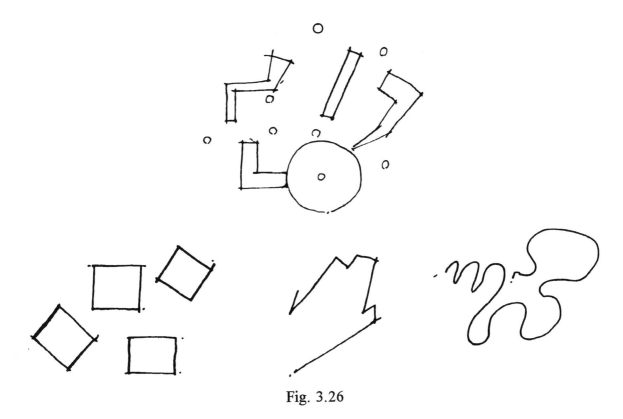

Fig. 3.26

Do these "corrections" of the shapes above create a better sense of harmony?

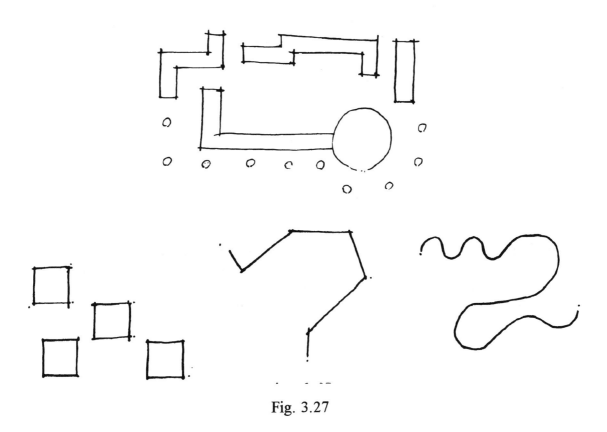

Fig. 3.27

You may want to think of harmony in design as a control over too much variety in detail. When variety is subordinated to an overall plan or concept, harmony may result.

Scale and proportion. Finally, we can consider scale and proportion as a kind of context criterion for a design. "Proportion" refers to the quantity relations of objects: for example, many bushes in relation to few trees, crowded (or bunched) perennials in relation to open spaces. We do not mean to suggest that many are preferable to few of anything; rather, we suggest that quantity relations must be considered to achieve a pleasing balance.

"Scale" refers to size relations: for example, large trees in relation to a small house. A designer must look at what exists and create designs that achieve pleasing scale relationships.

In this first sketch (Fig. 3.28), the tree is obviously way out of scale with the people if the site were for a house. (In a national forest located in the Northwest, however, we expect and relish this scale because it reminds humans of their minuteness in the scale of Nature and of our obligation to revere and be in awe of Nature.)

Fig. 3.28

In the sketch on the next page, the lack of proper scale and proportion should also be immediately evident.

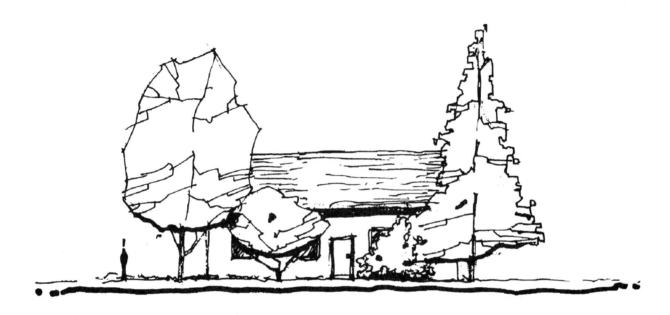

Fig. 3.29

In your design sketches, you are presently proceeding abstractly, without thinking much about what these sketches represent, so you won't be able to make a judgment about how scale and proportion relate to your own landscape design. But that consideration will come later, as you start creating your actual design.

* * *

In the next chapter, we show you how to make a plot plan that will include both buildings and planted areas on your site. Part of making such a plan is to know some of the symbols architects use to show certain common features. Knowing about them is also part of the preliminaries we explain in the next chapter.

Chapter 4

MAKING YOUR PLOT PLAN

As the term strongly suggests, a plot plan is a representation on paper of an area of human habitation. It is an accurate (remember scale?) drawing or map of a piece of property, which shows the precise size and location of most structures and vegetation. This can also be called "site analysis": taking a full and careful inventory of all relevant features of the site. This will include such matters as contours of the land, drainage, trees, and buildings.

You need to make a plot plan in order to assess both what you've already got in place and how you will change it. It will be the essential foundation of your evolving landscape design.

We're going to do this in two stages:
    1) plotting what is (explained in this chapter) and
    2) designing what should be (explained in Chapter 6).

The second stage, as you might guess, is the more complicated because it focuses on the future. Figuring out what can or should lie in the future strains politicians and normal people alike, but that's the fun of making your own design, as you'll discover.

***

Because your plot plan will include sketches of features of the site like walls, fences, and paving, you'll want to use recognizable symbols. So, we're going to show you several that professionals use. They're pretty simple, really.

<u>Property lines</u>. Assuming that you will want to demarcate the exact (or approximate if you don't have a surveyor's report) boundaries of your property, you'll use this kind of symbol for all sides:

Figure 4.0

Curb and pavement lines. If you want to show the present or projected placement of curbs and pavement, use these symbols:

Fig. 4.1

Miscellaneous utility features. Here are several symbols associated with lighting and other utilities that you may want to use:

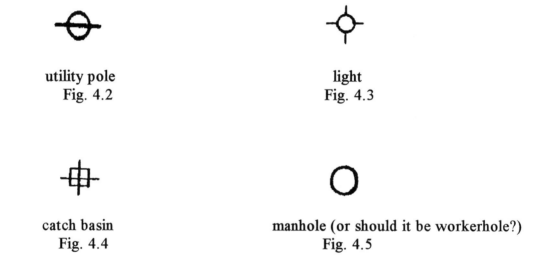

utility pole
Fig. 4.2

light
Fig. 4.3

catch basin
Fig. 4.4

manhole (or should it be workerhole?)
Fig. 4.5

Building symbols (e.g., house and garage). Outside walls are shown with double lines and to scale, with windows and doors differentiated from solid walls, like this:

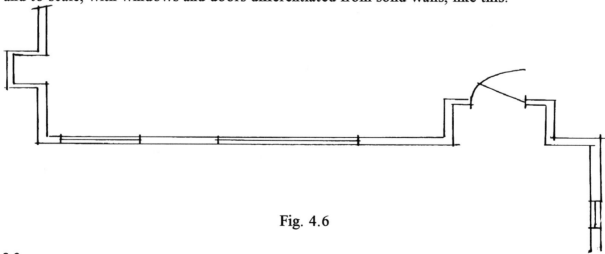

Fig. 4.6

Or the outline of the house can be simplified by using thicker and thinner lines. (Note that you will probably want to be sure you indicate window placement when it comes to considering views of and—perhaps—through your garden from inside the house.)

Whichever scheme of lines you use to indicate the building's "footprint," as architects call it, you must measure each dimension and show each part of the house to scale (e.g., 1" = 10'). As you will see later, if you don't stick to a scale representation of buildings, your landscape plan will be compromised.

Another feature of some buildings that you should show is roof overhang. (Remember that plants shielded from rain by this "umbrella" will need more of your attention than the rest of the garden.) Here's how you'll show that building part:

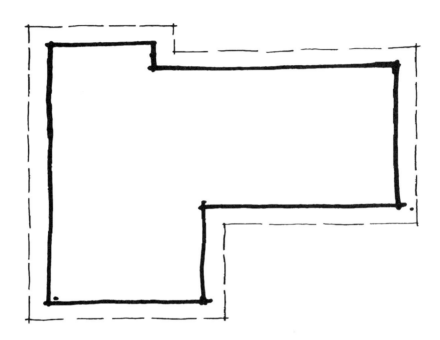

Fig. 4.7

Fences. The most common kinds of fences are wood and wire, shown this way:

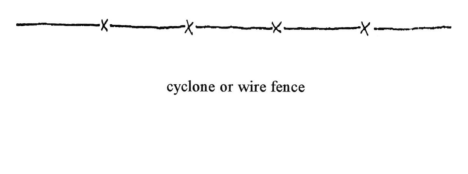

cyclone or wire fence

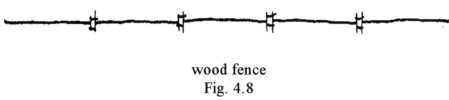

wood fence
Fig. 4.8

Walls. Stone and wood are the common materials used for walls:

rock or broken concrete wall

treated timber wall

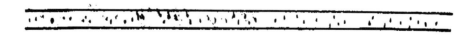

concrete wall
Fig. 4.9

Paving. Here are the symbols for various kinds of artificial ground coverings, such as brick and concrete:

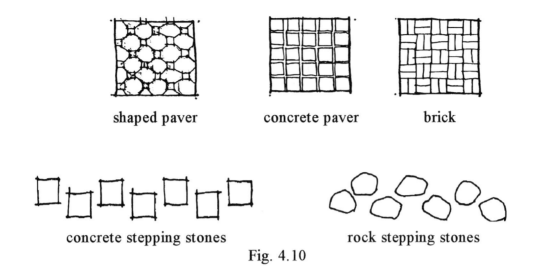

shaped paver   concrete paver   brick

concrete stepping stones   rock stepping stones

Fig. 4.10

Trees and plants. Presumably, there is some existing vegetation on almost any site you might be working with. Even though you may plan to add or remove a lot of it, you should show all existing trees and plants. Again working to scale (as closely as you can measure a tree's breadth or the spread of a shrub—its "dripline," as professional landscape types say), you will show either individual trees and plants like this:

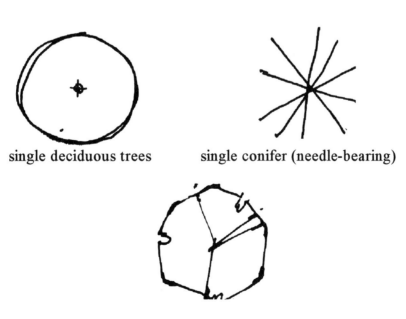

single deciduous trees   single conifer (needle-bearing)

single broad-leafed evergreen tree
or large shrub
Fig. 4.11

If broadleaf evergreens, like Oregon grape, holly, and rhododendrons, make up a clump of plants, show them this way:

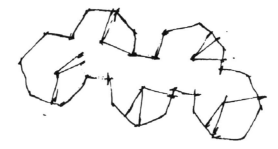

Fig. 4.12

Groups of conifers—such as pines and junipers—are shown with spiky edges:

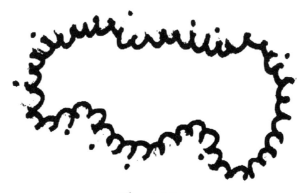

Fig. 4.13

Deciduous trees or bushes in a clump have a cloud-like representation:

Fig. 4.14

* * *

Following is a step-by-step procedure for drawing the plot plan of the little chunk of the world you're going to shape in your own image. Just so you can anticipate approximately how it's going to look, you see on page 36 a hypothetical plot plan (HPP), located in Anytown, U.S.A. Yours will look different, of course, but it will have many elements in common with this prototype.

STEP #1

Draw a reference from which to measure. Typically, this is the property line (the circled J on HPP—hypothetical plot plan). Since property lines are often invisible (unless accurately marked by a wall or fence), you may have to find out where yours are by asking the builder, by examining architectural drawings for your house, or by consulting your title insurance firm. Sometimes, none of these sources yields the necessary information. You might then confer with neighbors to see if they have good information about where their property lines are and therefore where yours begin.

If property lines are in dispute or you are otherwise helpless to know what exact chunk of earth to call your own (though we should all remember that in the broadest sense we are merely borrowing certain rights to the land; nobody really owns any piece of the earth), you'll need a licensed surveyor. Their services aren't cheap because their work is highly specialized, but you may have no alternative if you want to avoid future legal hassles.

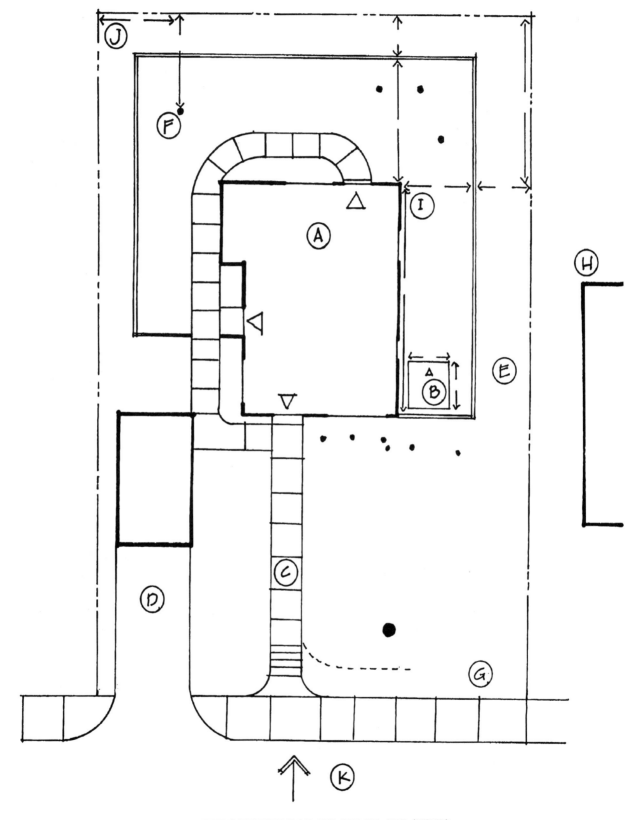

HYPOTHETICAL PLOT PLAN (HPP)
a generic sketch (like the mother of all plot plans)

When you aren't yet sure about precise property lines, you can indicate tentativeness about them by question marks. Measure out from certain points on the house to where you think the property line probably is as shown in I of HPP.

Notice that the boundary lines on all sides of the property are shown as alternating long and short lines to distinguish them from house lines, driplines, porches, patios, walkways, and decks.

So, you should now be armed with a common tape measure—preferably a metal one that has a stopper latch so you won't keep struggling to keep the damned thing from rewinding itself. Get out there and measure like mad!

Measure and record all the property lines, if you know exactly where they are.

If you're guessing where the demarcation lines are, measure from one side of the house to the property line and from another side to another property line. Start your sketch "in the field" with an approximate scale. You can refine it later when you've put the tape measure away and you're in a location more congenial to careful drawing.

STEP #2

Continue measuring along all the major structural features of the house, garage, and any other building on the site . . . the driveway . . . walkways . . . anything that would show up if you had an aerial photograph of your property. As you take these measurements, you can either list them as words and numbers in a notebook (e.g., "length of W side of house, 25'") or on a rough sketch that you make as you walk around the property, impressively flipping your tape measure about. (Your neighbors will surely be interested if they see you doing this. Conversations will almost certainly start, if they hadn't already, about what schemes you have in mind for enhancing the appearance of the neighborhood.)

Another detail to notice about taking measurements is dealing with corners of the property. If you choose not to measure in diagonally from a corner to some feature, such as a tree or part of the house, be sure you note the distance horizontally and vertically, as shown in F and J of HPP.

STEP #3

Be sure you measure all major plant materials—their size and location. And indicate any parts of the site that slope. Both the top and bottom of each slope should be plotted, along with the horizontal distance between the two and the height. Notice the dotted line between C and G of HPP for a simple way of drawing this feature. Also, while you plot the slopes, note any puddling in depressed areas; these probably unwelcome aquatic features suggests that you have a drainage problem, and it needs to be dealt with—later.

Also, because they have implications for plantings, locate on your plan principal utilities, especially the water meter, which will be involved if you expect to install an underground irrigation system.

Knowing where your electricity and/or gas meter and your telephone and cable TV lines are may also turn out to be relevant. If you have a septic tank, be sure you know where it and the drainage systems are located.

STEP #4

Bringing up the unpleasant subject of drainage problems does remind us and you that, while you are tramping around your site with tape measure, pencil, and pad or notebook, you will be noticing things—rather more scrupulously and minutely than you usually do. Unless you live on a concrete slab extending to the property line or in a townhouse with postage-stamp-size open space, you'll notice that your site has unique characteristics, some of which may better be called problems.

Ugh! Poor drainage. Too much sun. Lousy soil. No view or a view of telephone poles, garbage cans, and the back of somebody's garage.

Take heart. We're going to treat you to the irony that the problems are really the solutions. That is, you can study the problems, match them against your requirements, and make a plan that will convert the negatives into positives. The magic of good design!

Before we reveal the magic, though, you've got to take the repugnant step of recording the nasty parts of your site, as well as the things you like. As you do this, you should make notes that become a part of your plot plan; the notes, in turn, will become part of your design.

First, walk away from your house—across the street, down the block, across the meadow, into the woods, down the lane: wherever you can get an encompassing, contextual look at your property. Using new, unaccustomed eyes as much as possible—that is, observing your property as though you are seeing it for the first time, which isn't as hard to do as you might think—let these questions trickle through your mind and thereby guide what you see:

> What major elements of vegetation—trees, individual
> bushes, plant masses—harmonize with the architecture?
>
> Which of these elements set the house apart from others on
> the street or in the area?
>
> What elements conflict? For example, do large trees or rows
> of trees seem out of balance with other features on your site?
>
> What other structures that you can't change—such as water
> towers, telephone poles and wires, or city utility buildings—
> are inharmonious with your house and grounds?

Second, walk back toward your property. Observe closely the elevations of the land. Percolate these questions:

> Is the land flat or nearly so? If it is, does water stand
> on the surface (assuming fairly recent rainfall)?
>
> If you live in an unincorporated area, are there ditches running adjacent to
> your property? (Did you locate them to scale on your plot plan?)
>
> Does most of your property slope up- or downhill? (Consider
> slope beyond your property lines as well as within your site, and
> indicate it as well as you can on the plan.)

Third, try to identify the types of trees and major existing plants. If you're not fluent in plant names, you can get help from nursery staff, extension agents, or other arboretum or botanical garden staff. In the meantime, you can use approximate names or descriptions, e.g., 40' tall evergreen; bush with variegated, broad leaves, height about 6'. Samples of leaves, twigs, or bark taken to someone more knowledgeable than you about botany can also help you identify what vegetation you have.

Through studying your trees, especially, in this way, you will determine which you consider assets and which potential liabilities. Trees with soft wood can meet their demise and perhaps take part of your house with them in wind storms. Fast-growing trees like birches and other deciduous types produce roots that travel near the ground surface, with the result of lifting concrete sidewalk slabs and other paved surfaces and choking grass and other plants. These potential effects need to be charted on your plot plan.

Fourth (and this will require going away from your site or maybe just to your telephone), you need to check local codes and ordinances about fences or screens and storage shelters. Some municipalities forbid fencing or screening in front of houses; storage buildings usually may not be erected on property lines. Others do not allow tree removal or have lists of trees by type and variety that may not be cut down, or that may be planted.

Fifth, make a study of sights, sounds, and smells that may characterize your immediate environment, concentrating on whatever is undesirable.

What is the prevailing wind direction in both summer and winter?

Where does the sun rise and set in both summer and winter?

What are the locations of the chief eyesores, as well as the vistas you want to preserve?

Is there a likely source of unwelcome sound (e.g., industrial or commercial establishment, traffic)?

Do certain noxious odors regularly emanate from surrounding properties?

Include notes to yourself about all these intrusions on your serenity and sense of propriety. They will constitute your hit list when you start making your design!

* * *

OK. You've got all these things down for the first stage of your plot plan. Revealing, wasn't it? Who would have suspected that so many components of the environment impinge on our concept of how things ought to be? To preserve our sanity, we tune out much of what displeases us. But this time, you're going to take a proactive stance on most of these annoyances by creating a design that deflects them.

Chapter 5

PLANNING FOR CLIMATE CONTROL

In the previous chapter, we asked you to study your site with respect to prevailing wind direction and the sun's daily path. That was just a starter for what really needs to be done. Since these two determiners of climate are so vital to the ultimate success of your landscape design, we want to devote special attention to climate control.

The term may seem a bit of exaggeration, though. Humans don't ever really control climate unless they construct a biosphere—a self-sufficient, wholly artificially enclosed environment. When we all go to the moon or another planet to relieve population pressures on Earth, we'll know what climate control is with a vengeance. Meanwhile, we approach the matter with far more modest aims.

We define the term as follows: the use of building and plant materials to mitigate the worst effects of heat and cold and to maximize those most beneficial and pleasant to humans. Since we are primarily concerned with landscape design in this book, we emphasize the selection and placement of plant and other materials so that Old Sol, Mother Westwind, and you can exist in greatest harmony.

The terms of such harmony are somewhat different for each region of a huge country like the United States, of course. You can't expect a landscape design for a mostly arid and usually hot region to achieve good climate control equally well in one with a more moderate temperature range. So, the alert designer checks out the general climate characteristics of the region s/he is designing for. That shouldn't be too difficult for the long-time resident of a region; the experience of living there pretty much reveals typical climate patterns. For the newcomer, the public library is perhaps the best source of regional climate maps. The U.S. Government, for example, has published a wonderful wall map showing, in color, the various climate zones within each state and region of the United States (USDA Plant Hardiness Zone Map, U.S. Department of Agriculture, Miscellaneous Publication Number 1475, 1990). While such a map doesn't overtly say anything about sun and wind patterns, it does show usual temperature ranges and is therefore very useful when you select plant materials for a site.

When it comes to making crucial decisions for the site you are designing, you need some specific data arrayed so you can see them clearly. The information needs to take on prominence as you plan the smaller details of locating structures like fences and plant materials like trees.

Draw your preliminary plot plan from two perspectives—top and side like this (locating North accurately on both):

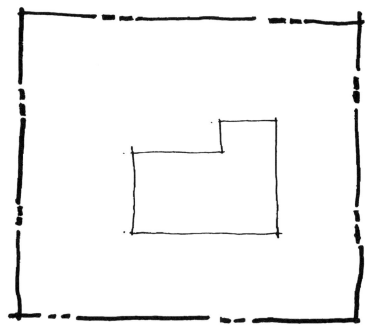

Top view of site
Fig. 5.0

Side view of site
Fig. 5.0 continued

Now, on the side-view sketch locate the sun's maximum altitude in summer and winter, and write down the average temperature range (either derived from printed information for your region or from your own recorded temperature readings over at least the first or last six months of one year). You can figure out the sun's altitude for your region by consulting an almanac. At 40 degrees north latitude (the location of such cities as New York, Indianapolis, and Denver), for example, the sun appears at noon on December 22 at an angle of 27 degrees; on June 22, it stands at 73 degrees. So, after you know the proper sun altitudes for your region, you'll show the winter and summer sun positions something like this:

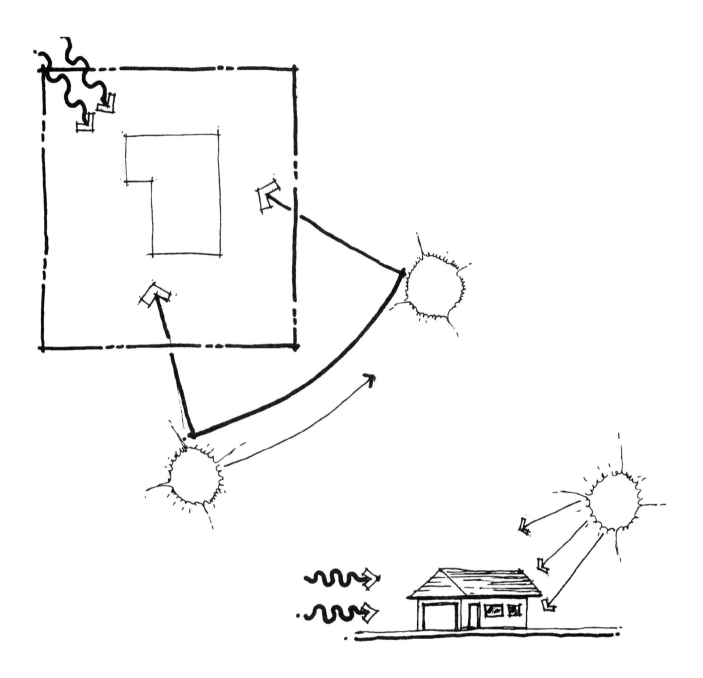

Fig. 5.1

Next, indicate on the top-view sketch the prevailing wind direction in both winter and summer. Remember that we speak of wind direction by referring to where it comes from rather than the direction it's going when it leaves us: a southeasterly wind heads northwesterly (unless it gets diverted). Show the wind direction like this:

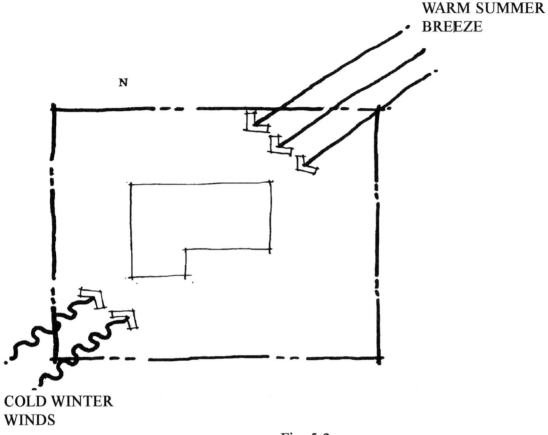

WARM SUMMER BREEZE

N

COLD WINTER WINDS

Fig. 5.2

If you are living at the site you're designing for, you may want to add notes to these sketches about your own impressions of climate. At one-month intervals, perhaps, you could go outside and sit or stand for a few minutes at the north, east, south, and west portions of the lot. Observe the sun as it appears—both its angle and its blocking by trees or other nearby structures. Jot down this information. With or without a moistened finger in the wind, note where the wind comes from and its intensity. Maybe a compass will help you be certain of the direction. You'll want to pay particular attention to wind eddies caused by built structures or trees. Do they seem to be significantly different from the prevailing winds? Make some notes about what you observe.

Some notes about how you feel in each of these locations at various times of year can also be helpful as you think about creating microclimates on your site—little enclaves where you will try to tailor-make the climate conditions to suit a particular use, such as vegetable growing or summer entertaining.

In making these observations, you may discover that some existing features of the house don't capitalize on sun and wind conditions. Windows may be too large in relation to the most direct summer sun; the doors may be placed exactly where they will admit maximum cold air.

Mitigating such unfortunate conditions may require extensive remodeling. Or, perhaps you can figure out through your landscape design how to compensate for them at lesser expense.

With this information compiled, you are in possession of valuable requirements for the conceptual plan explained in the next chapter.

Perhaps it will help you visualize the implications for your own site and design options to see several sketches of how plant materials can affect climate. Size, shape, foliage, and placement are the considerations.

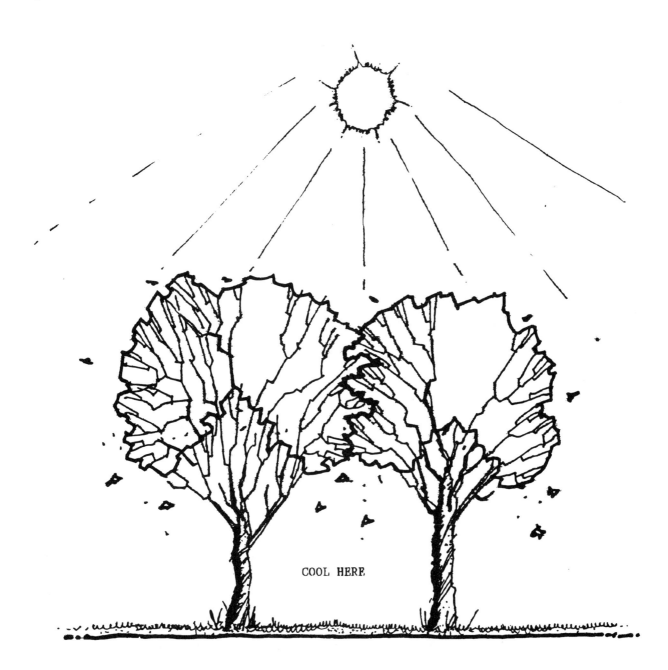

COOL HERE

Sketch #1
Large deciduous trees block the most
direct sun's rays and create cool spaces beneath

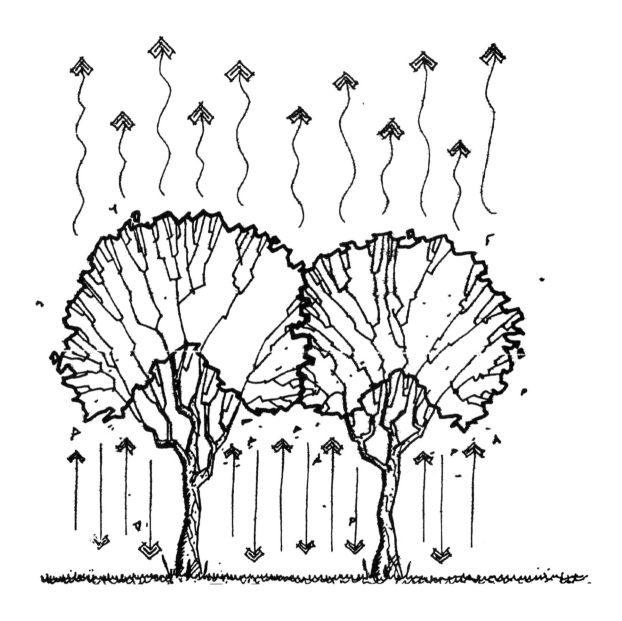

Sketch #2
Large deciduous trees absorb heat from
the ground beneath and radiate it upwards

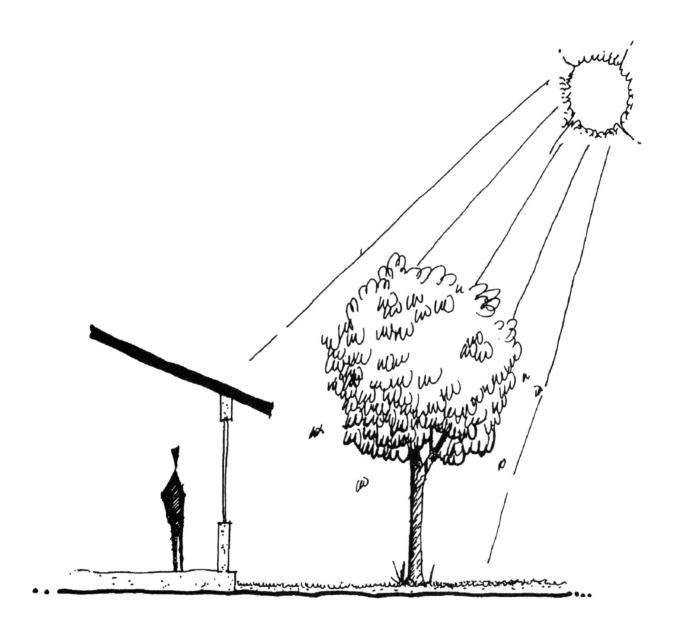

Sketch #3
A large, deciduous tree blocks direct sunlight
from entering a large window or from making
too much glare on a deck or other yard space
intended for people use

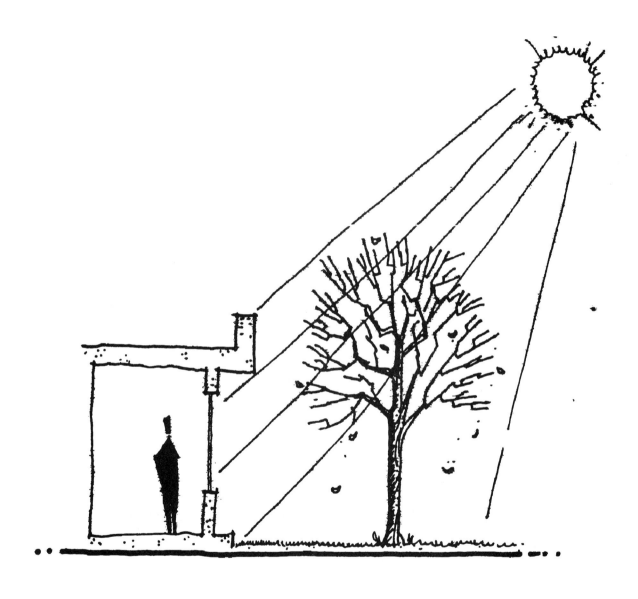

Sketch #4
A large deciduous tree, which has lost
its leaves in winter, admits sun's rays to warm
part of the house and yard

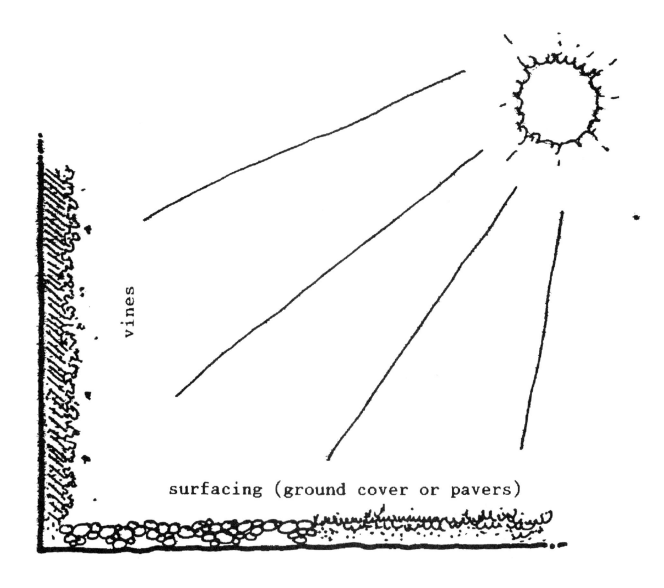

vines

surfacing (ground cover or pavers)

Sketch #5
Some surfaces (such as ground cover and spaced pavers)
absorb heat rather than reflect it harshly;
vines on walls or fences provide an insulating barrier
for a wall and a gently reflective surface on a fence

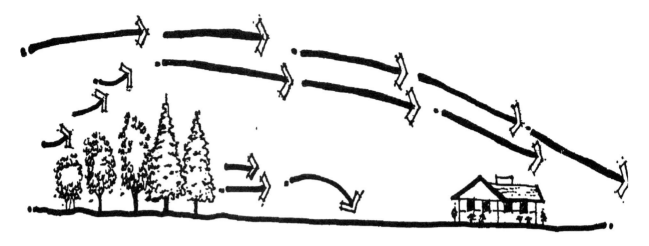

Sketch #6
Wind is deflected upward by a dense planting
of deciduous and evergreen trees, and air that gets through
is deflected downward

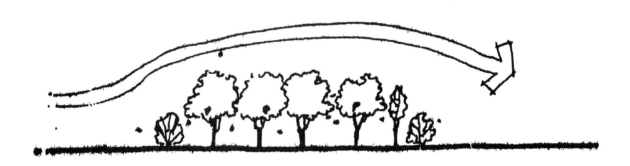

Sketch #7
Trees of more or less the same height cause wind
to move differently from trees of uneven heights

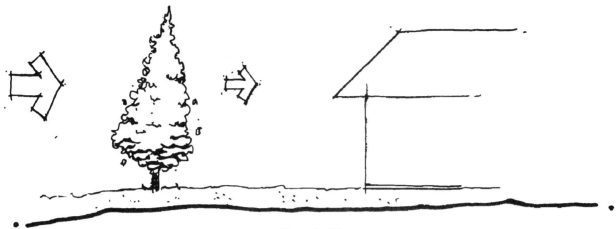

Sketch #8
**Even a single conifer can filter wind,
decreasing its intensity near a building**

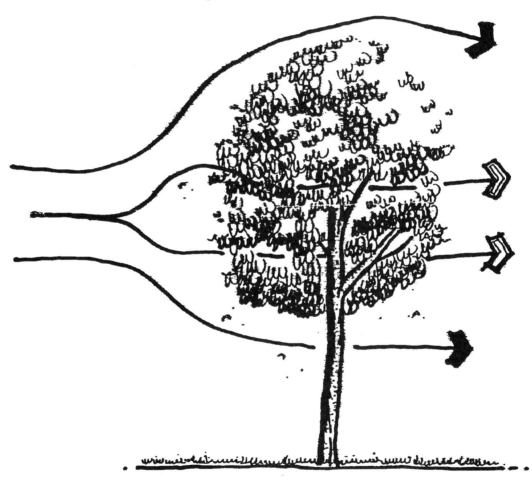

Sketch #9
**A large deciduous tree reduces the force of strong winds,
redirecting them to several different height levels**

Sketch #10
Even shrubs redirect strong winds to reduce their full force

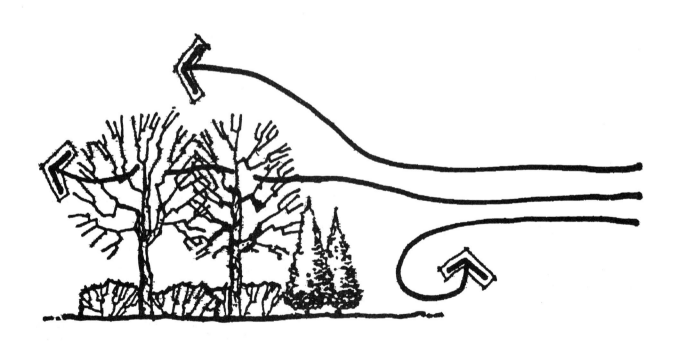

Sketch #11
Large deciduous trees in the winter, placed near evergreens,
filter and change wind direction, creating a less turbulent environment

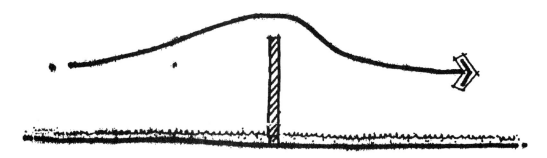

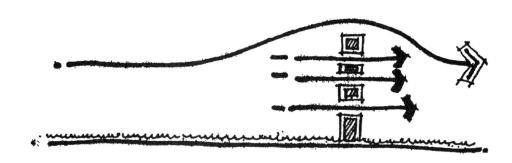

Sketch #12
Solidly constructed fences affect wind differently from
louvered or openly constructed fences

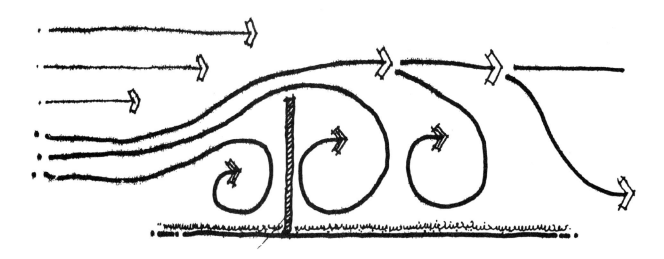

Sketch #13
A solidly constructed fence creates wind eddies,
which can make person caught in them feel uncomfortable;
an openly constructed fence avoids this problem.

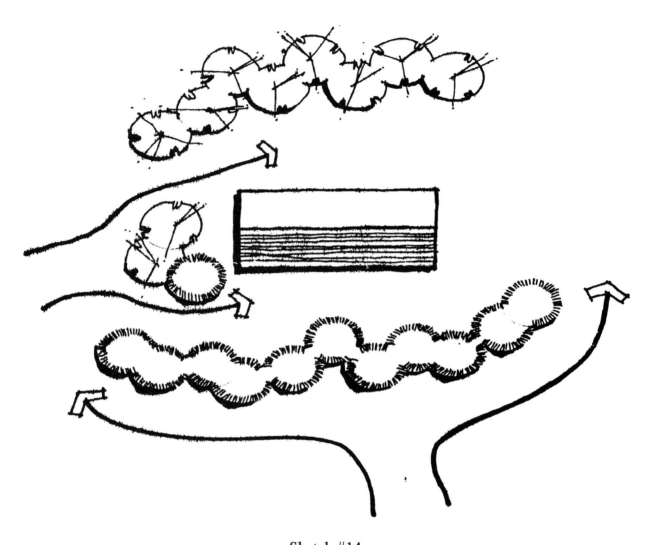

Sketch #14
Adroitly placed groups of trees and shrubs move the wind in several directions, protecting
the enclosed structure from the harshest blasts

Using these sketches as reminders and visualizations of the principles of achieving climate control, you may now be ready to think concretely about how you will use plant materials in your conceptual plan, which we undertake next.

Chapter 6

MAKING YOUR CONCEPTUAL PLAN

Your plot plan is before you: property lines, building footprints, major existing vegetation—all displayed to scale and in accurate interrelationships. You have made extensive notes about site problems and assets, varieties of trees and plants, local ordinances about fences and outbuildings, and other features of your site that have a bearing on its value to you.

Now it's time to use this plot plan as the foundation for your design process. Here, you will move from being a diagnostician of your property to being an artist: sculptor, painter, etcher, or whatever form of art strikes your fancy. Even if you've not drawn a picture since you were in third grade, what you will do next can reawaken some of the innocent joy you probably experienced as a child when you were involved in an art project. We want you to allow yourself that feeling because it will very likely help you discover design concepts. It's concepts we're after in this part of the process, not worked-out-in-detail plans for executing the design. You can let practicality (items like costs of labor and materials) intrude later.

* * *

You'll probably want to make several conceptual plans, both to try out various possibilities and to have a basis for comparisons when decision time comes. So, get at least a dozen pieces of thin sketch (or tracing) paper, the kind you can see through. (Most art supply stores have it, or you may be able to find a pad of usable paper in a variety store.)

Put a sheet of this paper on top of your plot plan, and either tape them together along the top or use tacks to fasten both pieces to a table or a thin, flat piece of wood or even corrugated cardboard.

What you will draw will be a "hypothetical bubble plan"—bubble-shaped figures laid over a plot plan, representing areas for proposed landscape treatments. To show you how these bubbles can indicate concepts, we present on the following pages one bubble plan for an in-city site and one for a more rural site.

Using the softest pencil you can find— you want broad, flowing lines, and you want to resist the temptation to depict fine detail—first freehand trace your property lines, the house and garage or carport footprints, and any existing features you think you want to preserve.

PLAN FOR IN-CITY SITE

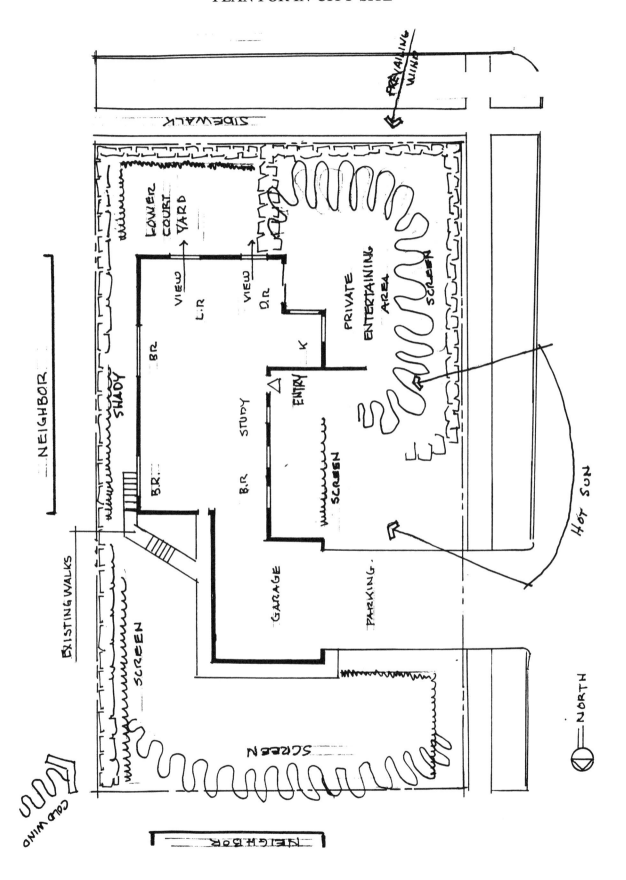

HYPOTHETICAL BUBBLE PLOT PLAN FOR IN-CITY SITE

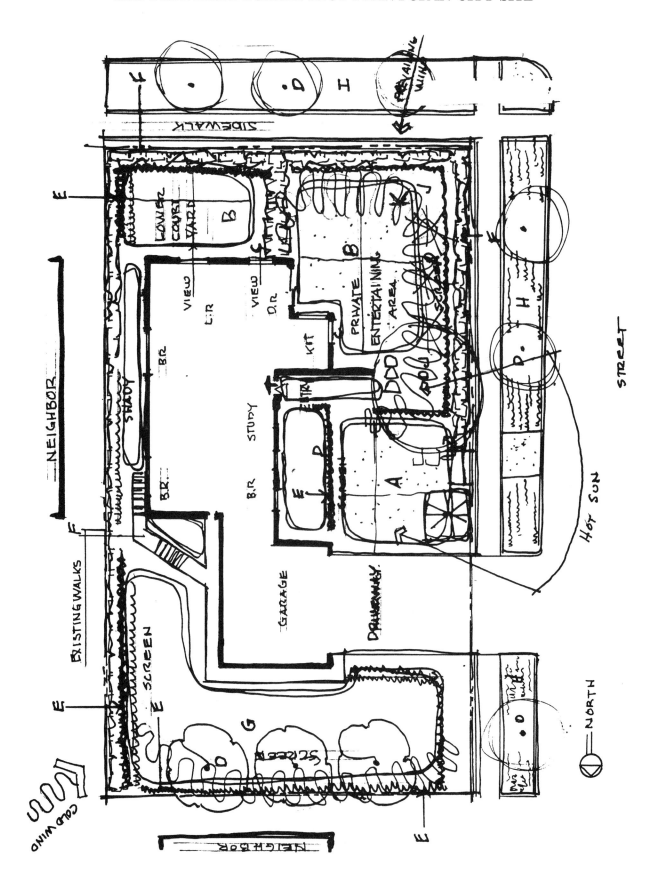

HYPOTHETICAL BUBBLE PLAN FOR IN-CITY SITE
(explanations of reasons for each bubble choice)

A = entry court—hardsurfaced for safe and
   easy walking and for low maintenance

B = sitting areas with privacy from street
   and neighbors

C = low-growing vegetation to frame and
   protect existing views

D = trees near street for shade and privacy

E = wood screen for privacy

F = existing rock walls and steps softened
   and made more attractive with evergreen
   plantings

G = small lawn for visual appeal

H = lawn in parking strip at entry side to make a
   setting for house (Alternative could be poured concrete
   and areas of ground cover for minimum maintenance.)

I = parking strip with ground cover and
   trees for durability and low maintenance

J = plant screen for feeling of enclosure and privacy

K = pool and waterfall for visual and sound enhancement

PLOT PLAN FOR COUNTRY SITE

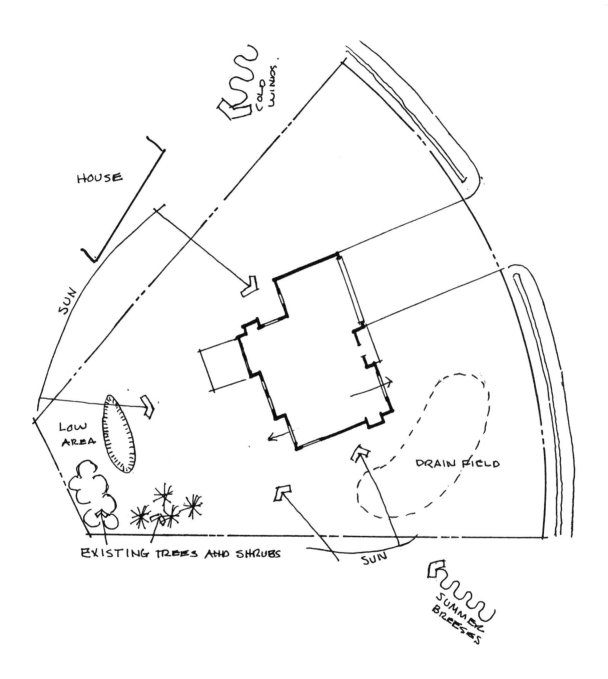

HYPOTHETICAL BUBBLE PLAN FOR PLOT PLAN FOR COUNTRY SITE

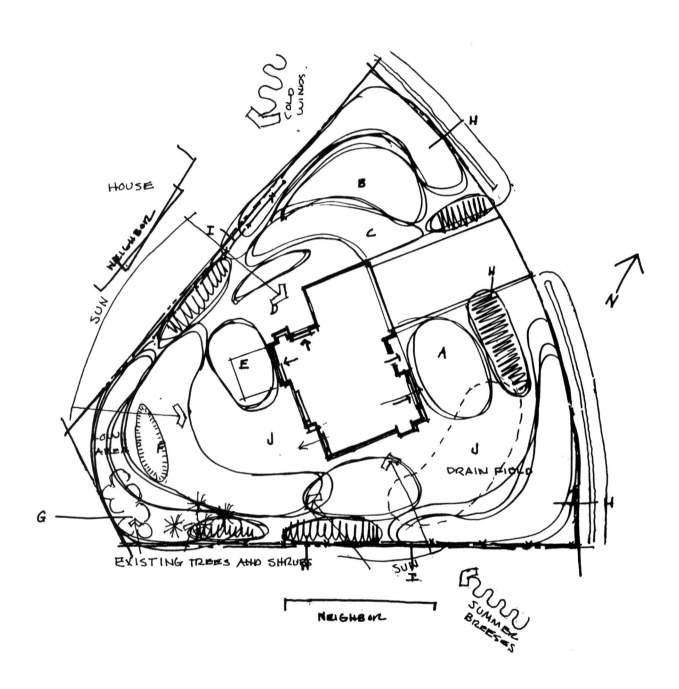

HYPOTHETICAL BUBBLE PLAN FOR COUNTRY SITE
(explanations of reasons for each bubble choice)

A = entry courtyard screened from street for privacy

B = dwarf grass or ground cover for minimum maintenance

C = oversized pathway for convenience in parking vehicles

D = courtyard visible through window at side of house
for visual beauty

E = patio with pavers or other smooth surface for
outdoor entertaining in season

F = meadow dwarf grasses, bulbs, and wildflowers for
ease of maintenance and low water consumption

G = native background screen plantings of deciduous and
conifer trees, also for ease of maintenance and low water
consumption

H = screen plantings for climate control

I = wood or wire fencing for privacy and against intrusion
by wild animals

At this stage, your conceptual plan contains the givens that you must or think you should accept. (Unless you plan to buy the lot next door or add extensively to the house, you're not going to be able to get away from these facts of existence.)

Next, using the kinds of bubbles/ellipses/circles you see in on pages 58 and 62, design the areas closest to the house. If the house already includes a patio, terrace, deck, or surfaced area, design around them. If adding such features is part of the future you hope for, indicate them in the approximate bubble method. When you are thinking about any of these areas, you will want to take into account sun and wind. You will probably want to capture as much of the former as possible and as little of the latter as you can manage. So, recall your notes on these givens of weather and let them influence your thinking about where to put the bubbles representing your extensions of living space into the outdoors.

Note that we have listed with our hypothetical bubbles some of the reasons for placing each bubble. We did this simply to demonstrate the kind of thinking process we recommend you use—one that accommodates the features of the site with the owner's expected needs and desires for living on that site. You, too, may want to include a few notes with each of your bubble conceptions to remind yourself later of what you were thinking.

Move next to other elements you might like to include: fenced or plant-screened areas, major tree or bush locations, open spaces to preserve or frame views beyond your site, perennial or annual beds, rokeries or small pools, trellises or other covered canopies, areas with a simple ground cover. This is not an exhaustive list of possibilities. As you recall what you have seen in pictures or at other people's sites, you can probably come up with lots of possibilities that might work at your site. This is why you need many sheets of sketch paper for many conceptual plans.

After you have designed at least a half-dozen configurations for use of the space, you'll probably realize you could go on doing this indefinitely. That's good. You want the feeling that your space has plasticity: it can be used in numerous different ways.

This sketching process should occur over a period of days or even weeks. Set each tentative sketch aside as you do others. Then, lay them all out on the floor or on a table. Each has its own potential value and usefulness because all display the givens, though each may suggest a very different way to deal with those givens. Nothing has been wasted in this proliferation of possibilities.

When the flurry of preliminary designing has subsided somewhat, select two or three of the sketches for a period of concentration. Lay them next to one another, apart from the others, and look at them with some design principles in mind: Where do you see repetition, sequence, variety, balance, harmony? You may have to stretch a bit to satisfy yourself that any of these principles is yet detectable in your conceptual plans, because you're still working at a pretty high level of abstraction. Nevertheless, you can probably find at least hints about how your bubbles are revealing unity in your preliminary design.

Perhaps these selective and comparative reviews of your sketches will enable you to pick a few—or maybe just one or two—that seem to have the most promise. Don't worry about foreclosing options as you make these selections. They're still tentative and you're not going to shred the rejects just yet.

On the sketches you've chosen as having promise, use your very soft pencil to draw a connecting line among all the loose shapes you've drawn. This line will represent a possible walkway system connecting all the use areas of your conceptual plan. The assumption here is that various kinds of foot traffic need to be accommodated: everyday approaches to the house and garage, service tasks such as depositing compostables and trash, and, certainly, the pure aesthetic satisfaction of walking among living things.

During the next few days or weeks, you may continue making sketches, adding to a now-impressive stack of conceptual plans. Twenty is not too many. How about fifty? During this period, ideas are cheap. Each new one may contain the seeds of the design that will be just right for you.

We wanted to take you just this far with design planning before explaining more of the details that eventually must play a role in finishing your design. So, the next seven chapters deal with specific elements or parts of most designs. Read with an eye to which of them may turn out to be most relevant to your situation. They include:

- streetside gardens and entry areas

- sideyards and corner lots

- terraces, patios, and decks

- small spaces

- play and recreation areas

- gardens: remodeled and from scratch

Chapter 7

STREETSIDE GARDENS AND ENTRY AREAS

Beginning with this chapter, we offer a series of focal emphases—parts of a landscape design that apply to most sites. But since each site is different, these emphases are not of equal importance to every designer. We suggest that you read through the next five chapters and determine which ones have greatest relevance for you. Then, you can select from these chapters the elements you need to incorporate in your design.

* * *

In this day of great dependence on the automobile for transportation to and from our homes, we can safely say that every house has a street side. (Maybe someday we'll have enough sense to switch to public transportation, walking or cycling between our homes and the transportation nodes.) Therefore, every landscape design needs to take into account what we might call the interface between site and street. Naturally, we think you should think of that interface as involving a garden or, at least, some kind of planting or set of designed features that creates for residents and vistors an aura of welcome.

One way to start thinking about how to create that aura is to observe its opposite: the all-too-common expanse of driveway and grass, with plantings crowded against the foundation of the house. We consider this popular concept—perhaps perpetrated by busy builders who wanted a quick fix but had no awareness of pleasing design—a certain recipe for boredom. Here's a sketch of what not to do:

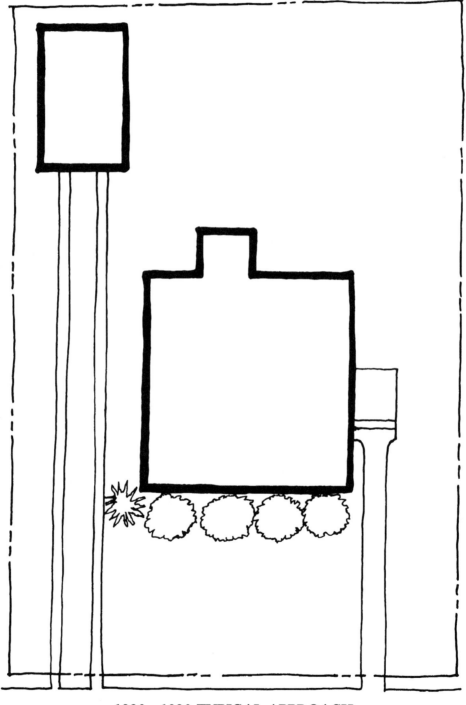

1920 - 1930 TYPICAL APPROACH
Fig. 7.0

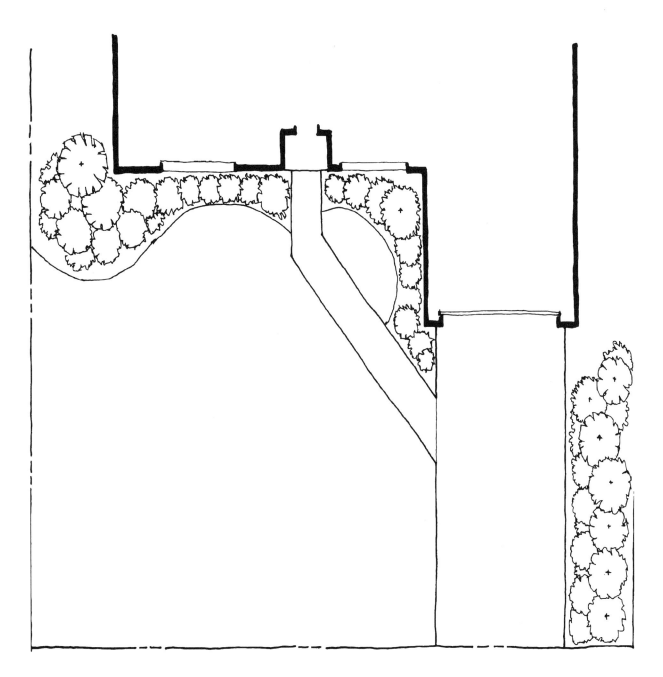

1970 - 1980 TYPICAL APPROACH
Fig. 7.1

Notice that in both the 1920s and 1970s approaches (Fig. 7.0 and 7.1) the driveway goes straight from the street to the garage, with open spaces devoted to grass and plantings bunched close to the house.

The placement and shape of the driveway are crucial to planning the rest of the streetside. A curving driveway is certainly better than a straight one—simply because curves are integral to Nature and offer more opportunities for interesting design. If there is any possibility of achieving that shape, it should be pursued.

A curving driveway is not only more graceful, most people agree; it also creates the illusion that the property is larger than it actually is. Further, the curving offers more possibilities for placement of trees, plantings, and other objects of interest. (Remember that Nature does not favor straight lines; they are entirely imposed by human planning.)

In determining the placement of the driveway, you need to know that the minimum width for a single lane is 10 feet, though it may be up to 12 feet in some cities. The angles of any curves will also need to be relatively small so that maneuvering a car will not become nightmarish and result in squashed plantings and dented fenders. Notice that in the following sketch (Fig. 7.2) the gently curving driveway and walkway allow for a circular treatment for the rest of the front yard and an asymmetrical placement of trees. The trees are accents for interest, and they also provide a visual reminder to change direction as a person approaches the house.

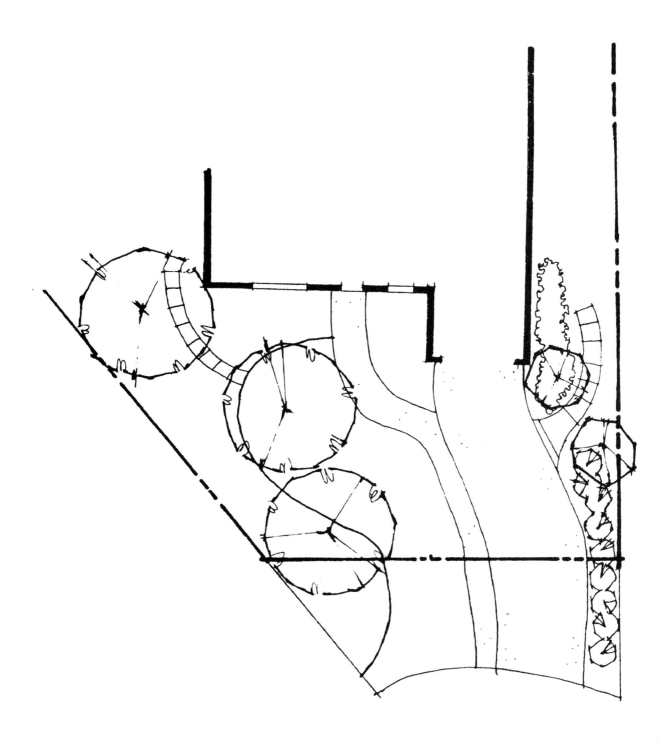

Fig. 7.2

   The scheme we have just proposed will be workable for many relatively small lots, where the house is fairly close to the street. For those sites where the house is at the rear of a large lot or where an easement allows entry from the street, there are additional difficulties in creating an interesting entry. Regimental rows of trees along both sides of the driveway or walkway can provide a stately, formal look. Or rows of trees and bushes of varying heights and spreads can help to avoid the feeling of an alley.

These sites will also require off-street parking, of course—as close to the front entrance as possible, perhaps also usable as a turnaround for the owner's car or cars. The next three sketches (Fig. 7.3) show three types of driveways with parking spaces and turnarounds. Minimum dimensions are indicated.

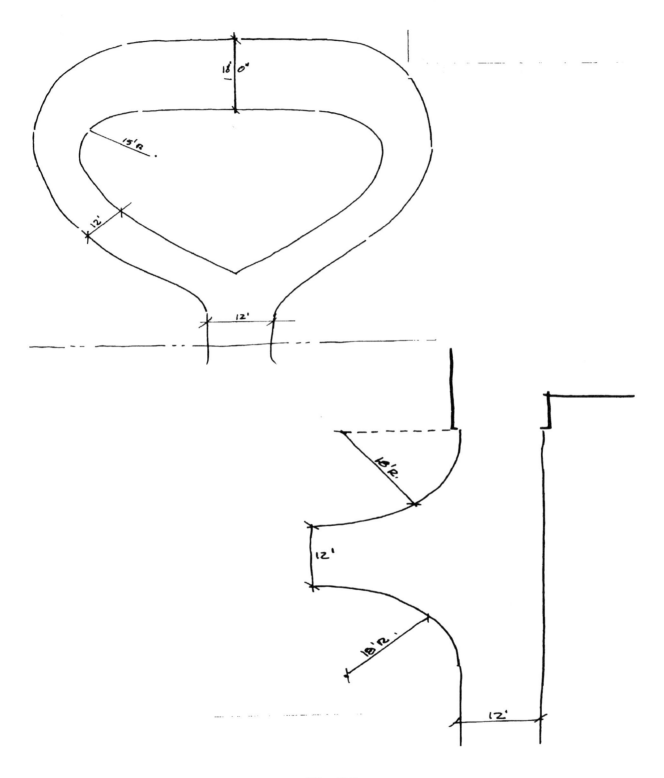

Fig. 7.3

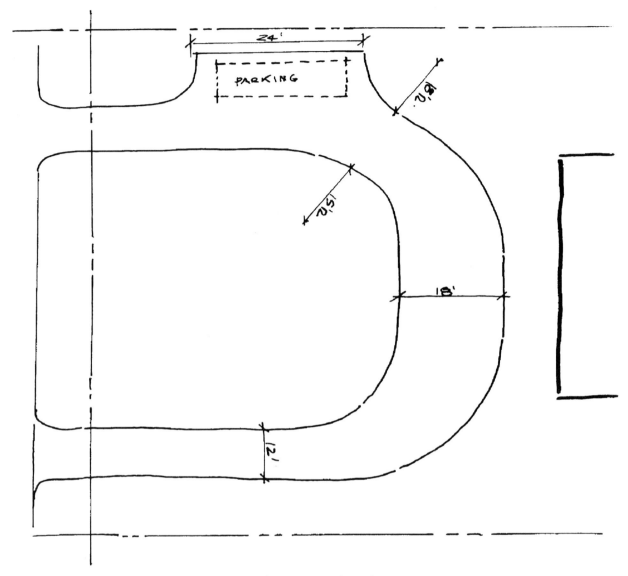

Fig. 7.3 continued

The following sketches (Fig. 7.4) show two ways of locating driveways and parking/turnaround areas for sites not close to the street.

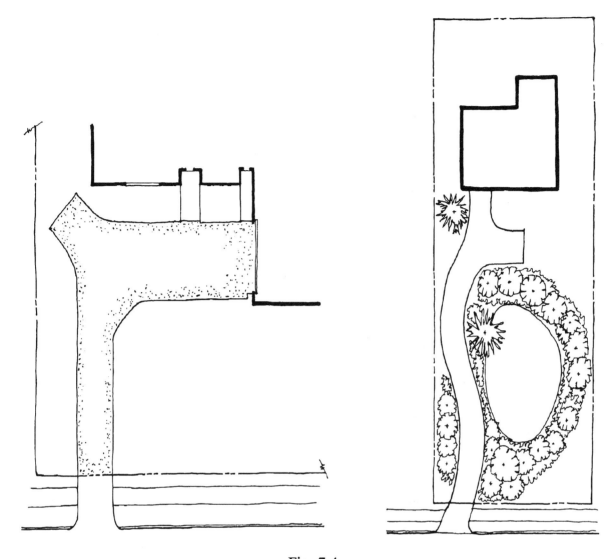

Fig. 7.4

As you saw in one of the sketches (Fig. 7.2) above, a walkway needs to be considered in relation to the driveway. In most existing neighborhoods and subdivisions, the walkways are too narrow. A test for adequate width is that two people can walk comfortably side-by-side. Major entrances for pedestrians from the street should be at least 54 inches wide. So, as you consider the placement and shape of the walkway, allow for greater width than you may now have. You might, for example, plan to add brick or stone along the edges of the existing walk or even another pour of concrete to widen the walk.

See the following sketch (Fig. 7.5), in which the driveway has been extended to each side and the existing straight-line walkway has been replaced by one that consists of graduated rectangular spaces:

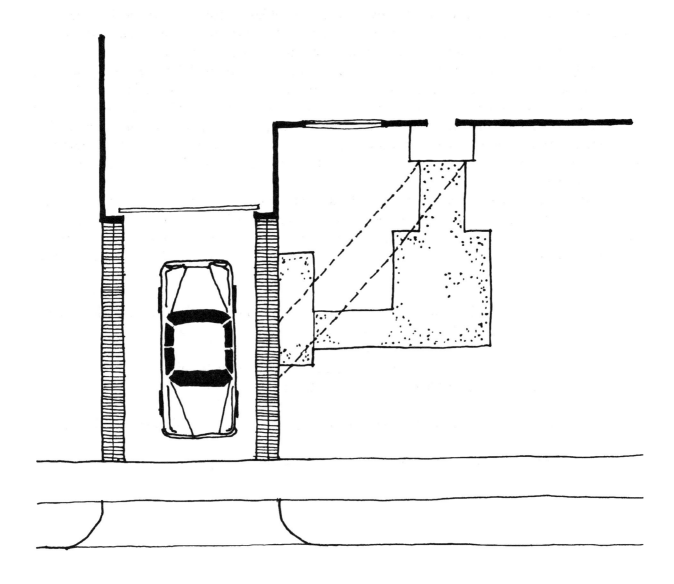

Fig. 7.5

The walkway also needs to be placed strategically. People getting out of cars parked in the street should not have to wander around, stepping on lawns or plantings to find the entry walk. You must therefore think about putting the walkway both where it will lead interestingly to the house (that is, with possible turns and pausing places) and where it will be readily accessible from visitors' probable parking places. Stand across the street and look at your site with that specific consideration in mind and then play around with placement on your conceptual design sketches.

While you are toying with possibilities for driveway and walkway, you should also think about vegetation near the street. Parking strips are often planted with grass, but ground covers are another attractive (and low maintenance) option. Some cities require that at least 60% of the parking strip be vegetation, so don't consider simply paving the whole thing with concrete. That may be the solution involving the lowest maintenance, but it's bound to be an awful eyesore.

Streetside gardens can include flowers and vegetables, of course, if planned so that they invite entrance and do not suggest merely an unkempt wilderness. (The wilderness may be Nature's way, but it won't work in present urban or suburban environments.)

Whether you will want to consider a fence along the street will depend heavily on what you are fencing out. If noise deflection or blocking of unchangeable visual blight are the motives, you can proceed with assurance. (Check for city regulations about how far back from the sidewalk or street the fence must be placed.) If you simply want to demarcate the property line or create a certain visual interest, you should proceed cautiously, considering fence height and materials in relation to the shape and materials of the house and to other design features that you will be contriving.

Walled or fenced gardens are especially desirable on arterials or busy city streets. While you may wish to enclose as much space as possible to create an interesting garden, we encourage you to plan a fence or wall setback of a few feet from the sidewalk or street, allowing for placement of greenery on the street side. Notice these features in the following sketch (Fig. 7.6):

A. On the street side, plantings leave the site open to the public, enhancing both the house and garden and the public space.

B. The space enclosed by a fence has greater potential for livability because it be comes more private and has reduced noise from street traffic.

C. The "inside" space can become a patio surrounded by trees, shrubs, and flowers.

D. A major walkway leads directly to the house entry.

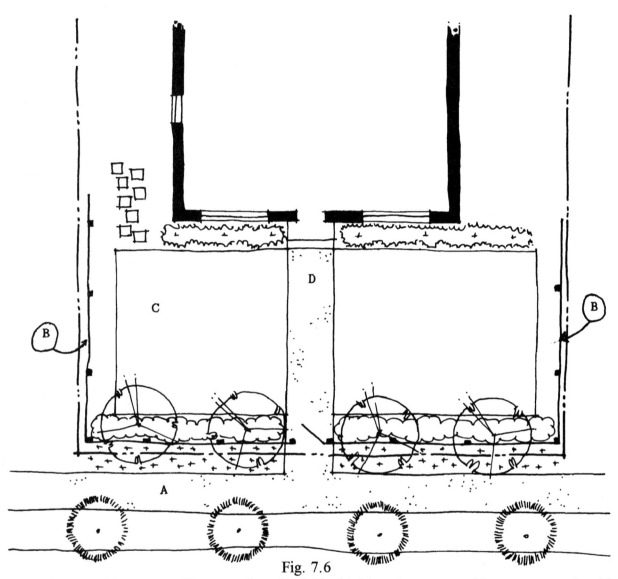

Fig. 7.6

Presumably, you readily agree that all of this thinking about streetside treatments should also be oriented with respect to the front door of the house. Remembering that the outside entry space (e.g., porch) should be level with the inside room or hall, think next about how you might extend that space and integrate it with the rest of the landscape design. A small existing porch, perhaps of concrete, can be covered with wood to make a larger porch or entry area. The owner thus creates better scale and enhances the functionality of a porch that was initially poorly designed.

If the house sits on a foundation that extends a foot or more above ground, steps are, of course, necessary. They must be at least 4 1/2 feet wide, with 6-inch risers and 14-inch treads. Knowing these minimum dimensions, you can calculate the total area of the steps needed for a particular site. Where the building entry is 5 or more feet above ground, groups of steps, rather than one long ladder-like approach, are desirable. You can plan, say, two groups of steps, with a landing between—a landing somewhat wider than the minimum 4 1/2—where a bench or plant containers can add interest to the entry.

While you're thinking about step design and placement, remember, too, that steps generally need railings, especially when more than one or two are involved. The railings should not seem an afterthought, and they should be substantial (no flimsy lath, please), in scale with the steps and the building, and preferably compatible as accent pieces for the house design. (Check for local codes on railings.)

We have looked at driveways, walkways, fences, and the front door. What about the space in between—what many people call the front yard but might more elegantly be called the entry court? Will it be an expanse of grass? A mixture of annuals, perennials, and trees? Front yards have typically been the least-used spaces around homes. They can be made into useful, livable spaces by applying a bit of imagination and ingenuity.

A first principle, we think, should be to create or preserve a view from the house to the street. The home is, after all, an integral part of a neighborhood, so the area around the house should be visually tied in. There should be a gradual transition between the all-business street and the protected home environment. So,in making your conceptual sketches of the area between street and front door, maintain a determination to blend driveway, walkway, and plantings so that you create the feeling of a true entry court—a place of temporary assembly, a place for greetings and leave-takings, a place that invites entry and lifts spirits. The following sketch (Fig. 7.7) may suggest a general idea for how this can be done.

A. Existing driveway and street provide parking for guests' cars and deliveries.

B. Addition of a walkway that changes direction adds visual interest to the approach to the house and allows for interesting use of "front yard" spaces (in this case entry to "interest area"—a small garden or sitting place).

C. Screens placed in staggered fashion provide privacy from the street without completely enclosing the space.

D. A small courtyard or interest area becomes a focal point as seen from inside the living room.

Plantings in all of the areas created by this design will, of course, enhance them.

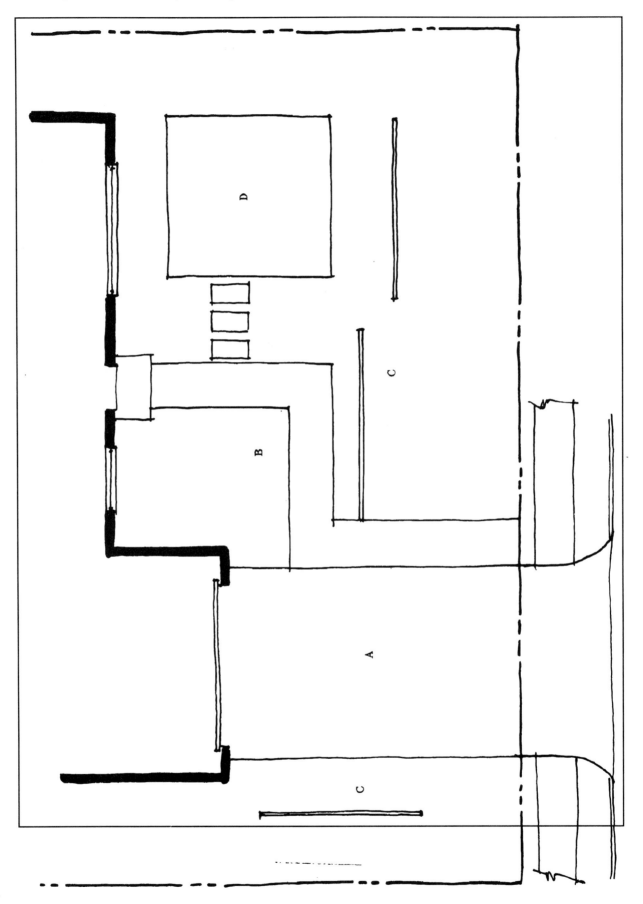

Fig. 7.7

Finally, a variation (see Fig. 7.8, page 82) on a street-driveway-front-yard treatment will suggest another of the many good ways of handling this common situation.

A. When the driveway is at the side of the lot, the garden designer has a larger area to work with. (We are assuming a house setback between forty and sixty feet from the street.)

B. Hard or soft coverings (i.e., pavers, bricks, ground covers) give the space a look of planned extension from the house—as if the original architect had planned the space this way.

C. A fence to enclose the courtyard should pick up or echo the house design and materials.

D. A focal point or interest area (perhaps with a feature such as a sculpture, fountain, pool, or rocks surrounded with bulbs and flowers in season) draws the eye of the visitor who enters the gate.

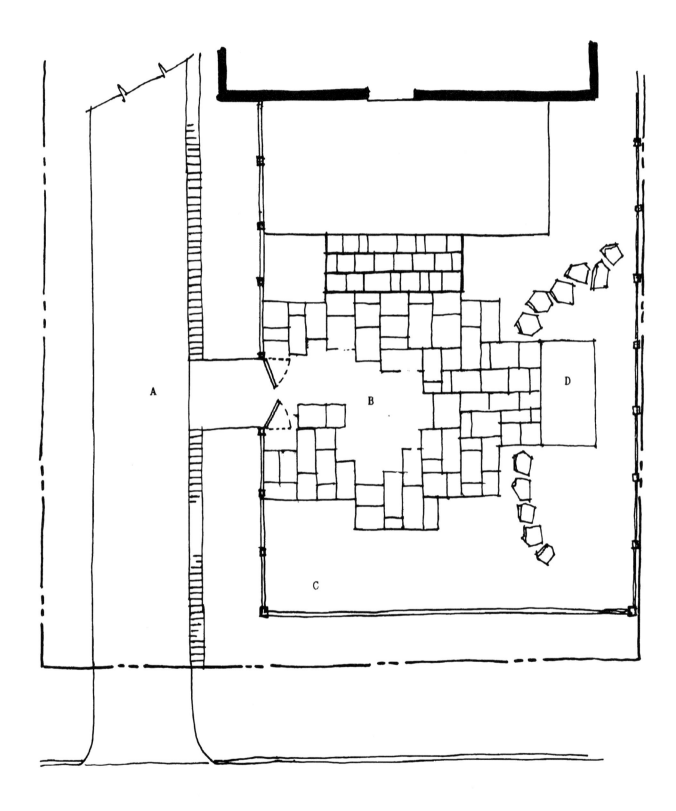

Fig. 7.8

A special problem with some city lots is a slope—either up or down from the street. What to do? Often, we see only grass, with no possibility of either privacy or visual appeal. In the following sketches, we suggest a few of the possible treatments.

In Fig. 7.9, the existing slope (curved line) and steps (dotted lines, representing a cut into only one part of the slope) are left intact and a fence defines the exterior line of the courtyard. Ground cover instead of grass on the slope decreases the difficulty of maintenance and improves its appearance.

Fig. 7.9

   The three-level wall shown in Fig. 7.10—made of landscape timbers or rocks and paralleling the front steps—can increase the amount of space in the courtyard and demands only minimum maintenance. A fence or screen at the top encloses the courtyard.

   A variation (Fig. 7.11) brings the wall to the streetside property line so that a fence screen can be moved forward, providing even more courtyard space.

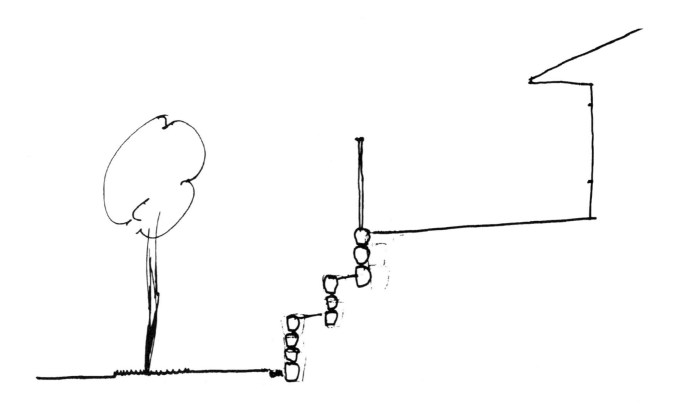

Fig. 7.10

Fig. 7.11

A longer-view sketch (Fig. 7.12) provides another perspective in which the lot slopes away from the street. Placing a wall close to the street obviously opens more of the courtyard to the view of passersby, whereas a wall placed closer to the house increases the screening effect while reducing courtyard area. A designer must decide which is more valuable: usable outdoor space or privacy screening.

At a sloping site where the space is sufficient, a meandering walkway from street or sidewalk to entry-court area may be a desirable solution. Indeed, such a walkway works best on a slope. As you look at Fig. 7.13, imagine the slashed line as representing a subsurface drain leading from house to sewer. The walkway roughly follows this line, with rocks (circles and ellipses indicating locations of either naturally occurring boulders or imported rock) placed so as to define curving portions of the walkway. Surfacing might be either very coarse sand ("turkey grit") or fine crushed rock or gravel. If done in fine attunement to the existing topography, this method of "taming" a slope can be both functional and visually stunning.

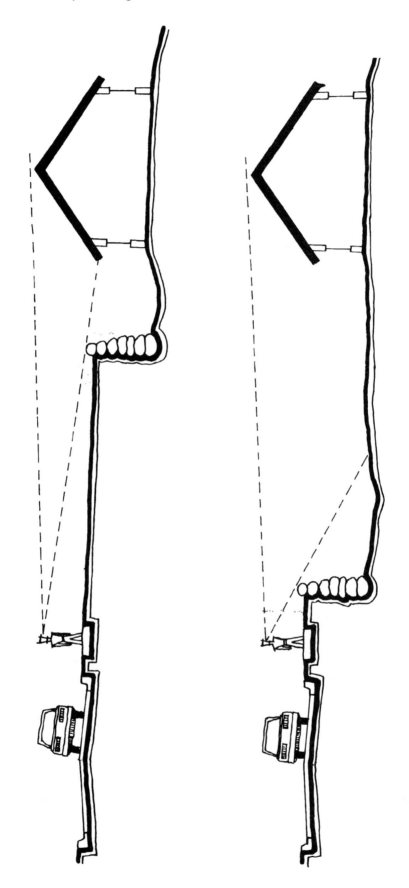

Fig. 7.12

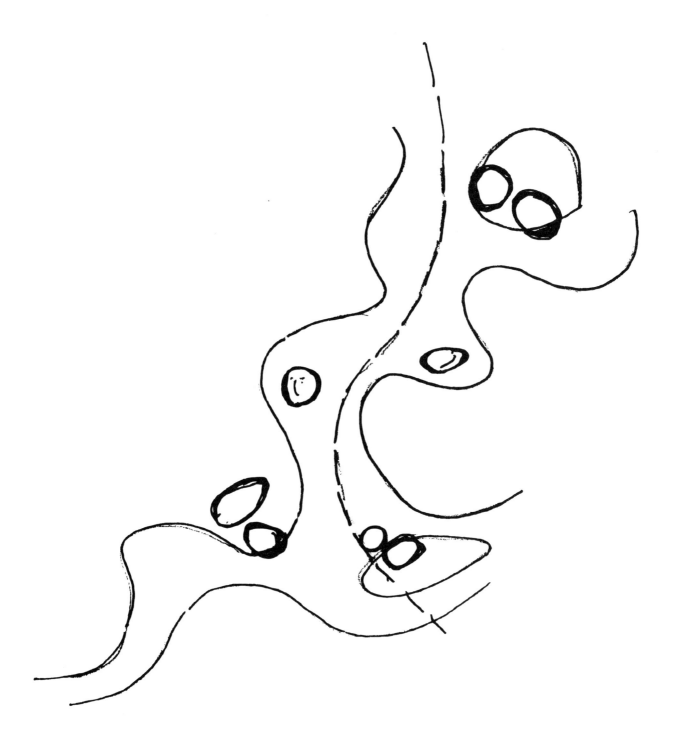

Fig. 7.13

Chapter 8

SIDEYARDS AND CORNER LOTS

Particularly in urban areas, where houses tend to be close together and where corner lots occur on every block, there may be special design problems. Will the sideyard space between houses be essentially "lost space," not consciously used for anything? Will the corner simply be outlined by a sidewalk and perhaps adorned with a bush or two? What can an owner do to reclaim these areas, if they are presently "lost," or to use them productively from the outset?

First, the sideyard. If the area is long and narrow, the dominant consideration is to design a walkway that will minimize the tunnel look and will allow for plantings and perhaps certain forms of entertainment. Following are two sketches of walkway ideas: the first (Fig. 8.0) a pathway among raised vegetable bins or storage and compost containers; the second (Fig. 8.1) a curving walkway that meanders among trees or bushes.

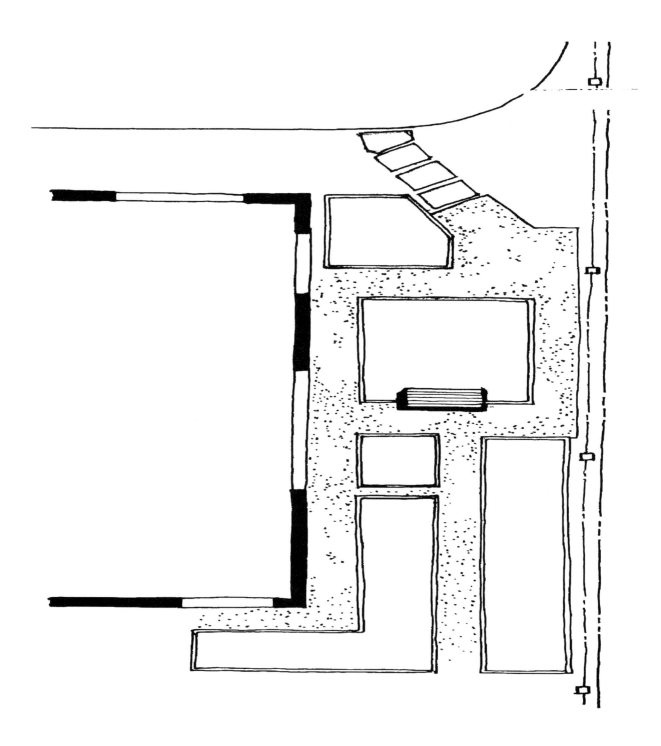

Fig. 8.0

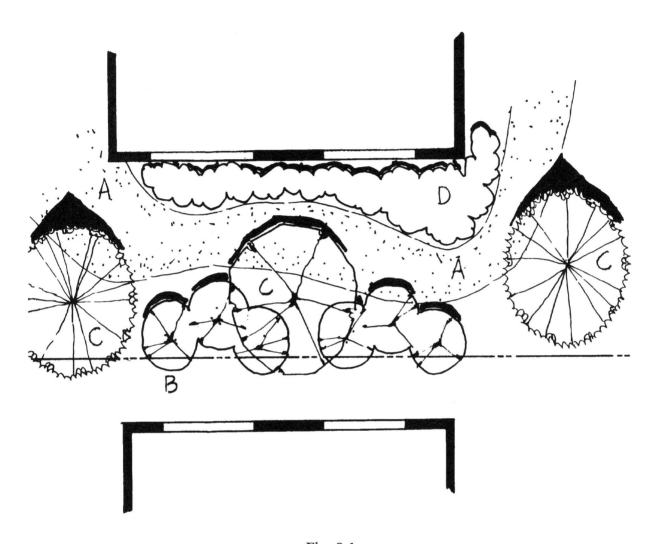

Fig. 8.1

A = pathway—fine, crushed gravel or bark
B = property line
C = screen planting—trees or bushes
D = low base planting—shrubs or perennials

    Notice that each of these basic ideas immediately opens options for creating almost year-round uses for such space. If the land slopes, some such treatment as a rockery, wall, terrace, or deck will be necessary to hold the soil in place and to create an area that is level enough to permit placement of a stable walkway, planter boxes, or whatever other features may suit the area.

Depending on what is next door on either or both sides, you may want to consider some visual screening for privacy. This is best achieved through cooperation with neighbors, so that both sides of the screening are visually appealing through all seasons. A lattice fence or trees or shrubs that are upright in form and evergreen are first choices. Tall deciduous shrubs that can be kept pruned laterally will assure that plants will not grow out of scale to the space. The following sketches suggest how these choices might look:

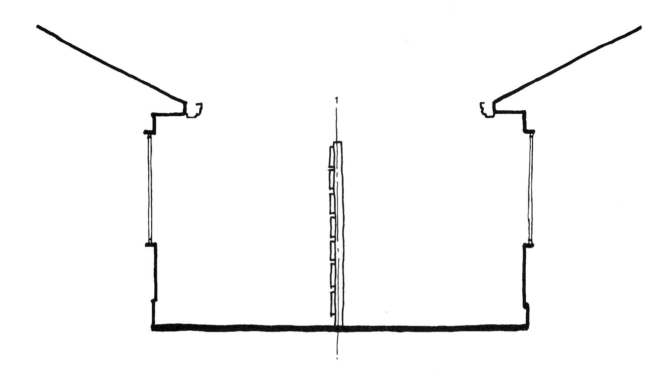

Fig. 8.2

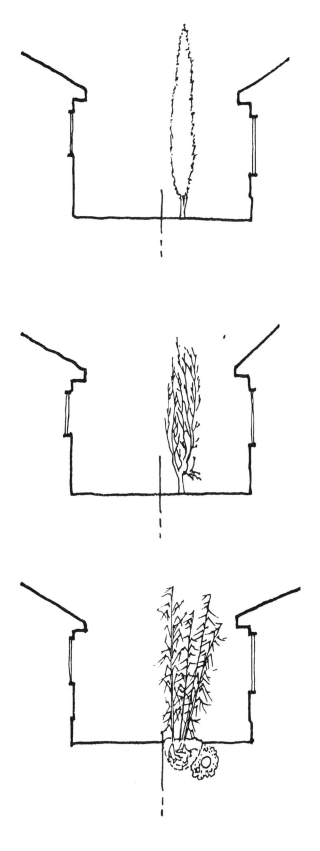

Fig. 8.3

A sideyard is also a good place to establish a microclimate—an area that gets continuous sunshine through much of the summer and winter day and is protected from cold winds. Locating structures such as fences and the right kinds of trees and bushes will create a microclimate, which might occupy 8 to 15 feet of the sideyard. The specific location might be oriented on a window, so that whatever you place in the area will also be enjoyable from inside the house. Within the area might be a bench, table, small pool, deck, trellis, rock grouping, or sculpture. Play structures and game areas for both children and adults can also be adapted to these microspaces, though scale must always be considered carefully.

If growing vegetables or flowers is an attractive possibility, you may wish to incorporate a coldframe or hotbed to grow seedlings, cuttings, or plant divisions for later transplanting. No space is too small for these purposes.

When the sideyard faces north, a "native garden" may be the best choice: a selection of plants native to the region and that require no special sun conditions—trees, shrubs, mosses, cacti, groundcovers, flowers. As you think about placement of several of these forms of vegetation, consider your curving pathway. Heavy-textured plants or unusual shapes should be at turns in the path; smaller or less-dense plants should alternate. Plant size is crucial for this purpose. Avoid plants that you know will outgrow the area.

Corner areas, where the lot is bordered by two streets that come together in an intersection, require special care in landscape design. Not only are they conspicuous to all passersby—and therefore should be visually appealing—but also are they potentially dangerous. If the plantings block drivers' views, the site owner is at least indirectly responsible for collisions that may result. As Fig. 8.4 shows, an imaginary arc around the corner of the lot should guide the design.

Any trees or shrubs that are likely to grow tall should be placed toward the rear of that arc—pulled back from the corner. However, that consideration need not limit other design ideas. Fig. 8.4 suggests one rather simple plan.

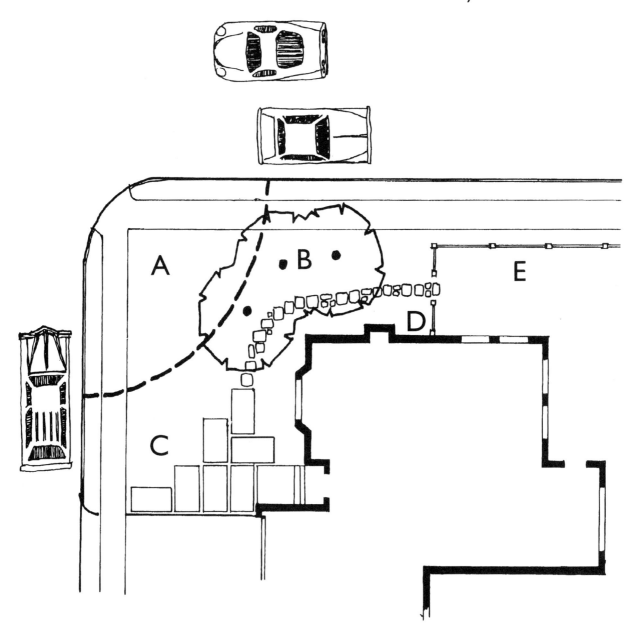

Fig. 8.4

A = area kept free of view-blocking structures or foliage
B = trees or bushes marking frontscape from rear
C = setbacks with ground cover or dwarf grasses
D = curving pathway connecting front and back areas
E = fence located so that it does not connect at the corner
    of the house

Chapter 9

PATIOS, TERRACES, AND DECKS

In some parts of the United States, a deck is almost an obligatory feature for middle- and upper-class homes—a status feature, an expected adjunct of everyday living, at least during pleasant weather. If it's not a deck, then it might be a patio. In fact, the word "patio" has become so generalized in meaning that it can apply to almost any exterior space devoted primarily to recreation. So, we see barbecue outfits, bicycles, camping gear, even RVs located in what passes for a patio.

At one time the word "patio" meant a courtyard surrounded on at least three sides by walls or columns—an enclosed, protected space that was, in effect, a part of the house. And "terrace" meant a level paved or planted area adjoining a house, usually not surrounded by walls. Now, the meanings of all three words—"deck," "patio," "terrace"—seem to have become blurred and blended into more or less the same thing. All refer to an extension of a house or other building, intended to serve recreational or entertainment purposes.

If a deck/terrace/patio is going to have high priority in your landscape designing, you need to know certain minimum specifications or criteria:

1. <u>Size</u>. The number of people who will be using the space regularly should determine its size in square feet. Seventy-five to eighty square feet per person have generally proved a reasonable estimate. If frequent entertaining is likely, the area could well be greater—up to the maximum that the site will allow, both aesthetically and according to local building codes.

2. <u>Location</u>. While it may go without saying that the deck/terrace/patio will be adjacent to the house, some sites may require a bit more detachment, perhaps to take advantage of sun, shade, or view. Avoidance of strong, unpleasant winds may also be a consideration. The ideal location—at least in sections of the country with a temperate climate—is the southeast side of a building because it will get morning and mid-afternoon sun in all seasons. For most people, the play of sun and shadow has a pleasing effect—shadows created by trees, an umbrella, or other simple structures. In more torrid climates, of course, the coolest side of the building is the obvious choice for an outdoor living area. Screening may also be necessary in some locales.

See the following sketch (Fig. 9.0) to help visualize a few main criteria for location. Notice the location of the midday sun, the direction of prevailing summer winds, and the placement of plant materials to make this small extension of the house most usable. (The small square box set on the deck is for low-growing plant materials.)

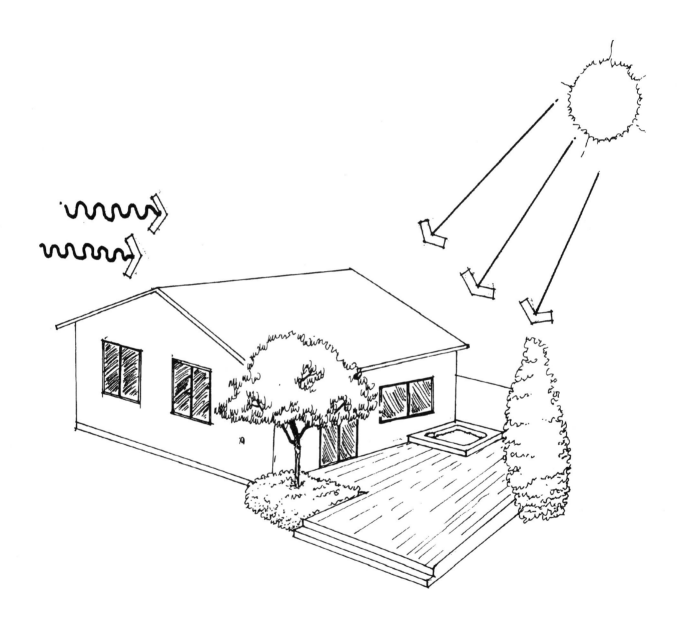

Fig. 9.0

3. <u>Shape</u>. Simplicity is the key criterion here. Rectangles or squares should predominate, though, as the previous sketch (Fig. 9.0) shows, one side of the rectangle might well altered to accommodate the available space, access from the building, or an existing tree. Also, expected use should condition the shape, especially the part of the area where people and pet movement will be heaviest. Sitting areas should obviously not obstruct traffic flow. Who wants the golden retriever's tail brushing the pizza all summer?

4. <u>Materials</u>. The surfacing material for a patio or terrace needs to be in design harmony with the rest of the garden. It should also be consistent with the style of the house and the overall type or mood of garden design (e.g., "natural," contemporary, traditional, etc. See Chapter 12.) The following sketch (Fig. 9.1) displays several of the possibilities as a composite—though not with the intention that so many materials should be combined in this way.

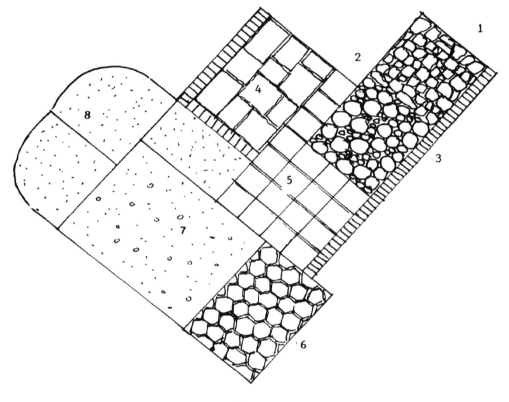

Fig. 9.1

1 = pieces of quarried flat stone laid by
      hand on bed of sand with good drainage
2 = flat river rock set with very little
      space between each rock

Note: 1 & 2 make placement of chairs
      and tables somewhat difficult.

3 = edging of bricks, set either on sand or in
      concrete

Note: #3 is especially good in
      traditional gardens.

4 = flagstone or slate laid on concrete
(never on sand or crushed rock)

5 = precast concrete pavers ranging in size
from 12" to 24" square

6 = precast hexagonal pavers laid dry or on
concrete

7 = poured concrete with large exposed gravel
aggregate

8 = pea-gravel exposed aggregate

Note: Smooth concrete—contrasted to
broom-finished, as in city sidewalks—
is never used outside because it is too slippery.

For people on a very limited budget (the materials suggested above <u>can</u> get expensive), a mixture of existing porous, sandy soils and cement yields a reasonably durable surface. This technique is suited, however, only to areas where no danger of deep frosts exists, and it is best attempted only after consultation with people in the cement business.

Before you make a decision about the surfacing for a patio, you should visit completed gardens to see a variety of surfacing materials. Consider both their suitability for the rest of the garden design and the likelihood that they will function well for your outdoor living needs.

Decks are usually constructed of wood—cedar, redwood, or treated fir or pine. The more complicated the deck's shape, the more difficult the construction, of course, so simplicity is advisable. Long flights of steps should be avoided, too, because they are monotonous and difficult to navigate. A maximum of six to eight steps is recommended, preferably with some change in direction. The bottom step should lead directly to a feature—such as a path, sitting area, or garden feature—to which you want to direct people.

Chapter 10

SMALL SPACES

For people who live in condominiums (where, it is true, much of the landscaping is often done by others), apartments, or houses on very small lots, landscape design is still possible. The difference is scale: thinking small. The difference is also in placement of objects: a few objects that will define space in ingenious ways.

One of the most useful precedents for this approach to landscaping is the Japanese model. In essence, that theory consists of dividing the whole space into smaller units using vertical plantings: vines on wire or wood trellises, walls of green plants in containers, or hanging baskets with plants that trail to the floor.

Figure 10.0 shows a single vertical plant wall, with a small section of low-growing plants in front and taller plants stretching to the maximum possible height for the space. The base for this wall is non-rusting wires attached at bottom and top or possibly even chain link fencing. Climbing vines or grasses placed against this wall eventually cover it, hiding the support.

Fig. 10.0

Figure 10.1 shows a scaled-down version of a vertical plant wall—this one consisting of wooden or metal posts set in a portable wooden box, with wire strung between the posts.

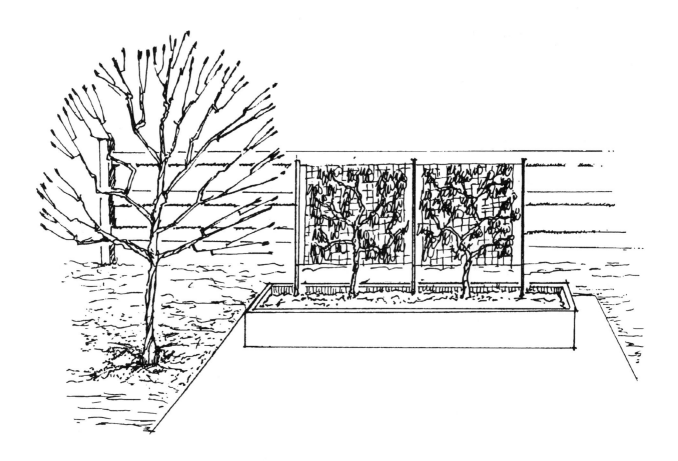

Fig. 10.1

These vertical plant walls can provide both a screen from close neighbors or from undesirable views and a background for other design features.   In Figure 10.2 a built-in bench abuts the plant wall, providing seating space for three or four people within a partial enclosure.

Fig. 10.2

This view from the interior of the building to the exterior small space illustrates the integration of both areas, the small space becoming an extension or projection of the interior. In achieving this integration, the designer also makes the small space seem larger.

Another design device that nearly always helps to achieve this illusion is the use of two or more levels. By incorporating actual steps (flat rock, wood timbers) or an inclined path in the design, we add just enough complexity to the small space to pique interest. Figure 10.3 (in three variations) illustrates a typical narrow space between house and property line—a kind of small space that is often difficult to make appealing. The row of pyramidal evergreens at the left defines the space. The upper level also has a vertical plant wall to define its other outer limit. In order to keep the rest of the space from seeming a hallway or alley, two steps divide the two sections, with a couple of shrubs to further punctuate them. The areas thus defined can then become useful for seating and can have more plants to suit the seasons and the users' preferences.

Fig. 10.3

Fig. 10.4 shows a similar space, seen from a top view: a larger, planted divider and stepping stones (or a small sloping path) both dividing and unifying a series of areas within the subdivided small space.

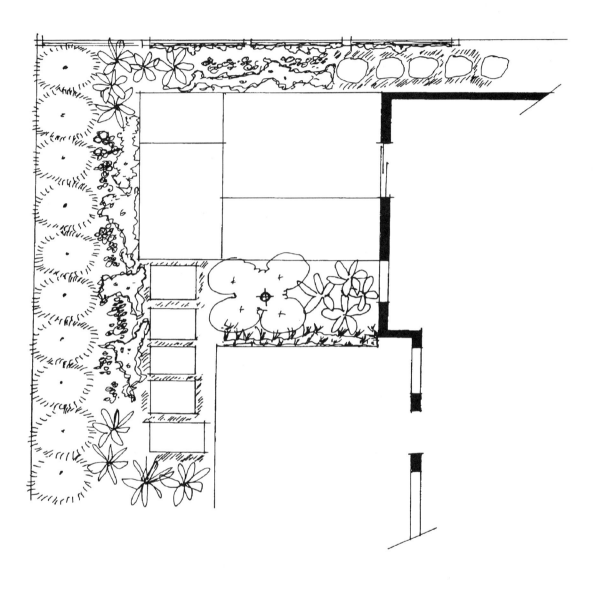

Fig. 10.4

Finally, in Figure 10.5 a deck similar to many that are part of condos becomes an out-door room, with a planter tub and a table protruding from the wall to break up the open-square look. Decorative plants act as desired to give the space a feeling of a garden room.

Fig. 10.5

Chapter 16 deals with many choices of trees and plants involving size, shape, and texture of foliage. These choices will be especially critical in detailed designing of small spaces because scale and proportion become so prominent.

Chapter 11

PLAY SPACES FOR CHILDREN

Especially during their younger years, children's outdoor activities should play a role in landscape design. True, many children can play games or otherwise entertain themselves in an untended meadow or a patch of dirt. They don't necessarily need consciously designed play areas, with elaborate equipment (such as hand-hewn timbers, artfully joined by rope and pegs to make an impressive climbing/swing/slide structure). However, enough parents want their young children to have designated play space and equipment— if only for reasons of safety and supervision—to make this a fairly high priority.

The clever landscape designer will therefore consider children's uses of all or part of the area adjoining a house, thinking both about short- and long-term uses of that area. When the children are older or involved in different kinds of activity, wouldn't it be nice to have a plan for other uses? And shouldn't that plan make the transition from child uses to adult uses easy and efficient?

We suggest the following as feasible and versatile possibilities for convertible play spaces: groupings of rocks, sandboxes, hill-climbs, pools, free-standing upright logs, and wire columns. We hope they will stimulate you to come up with other imaginative, relatively inexpensive solutions to the problem of designing for children.

Rock groupings. Large rocks or boulders, often discarded by house builders, can make intriguing invitations for children to climb. Since suitable boulders can weigh from several hundred to several thousand pounds, their use depends on assistance in placement.

As Figure 11.0 shows, either one large boulder (two or three feet high) or from three to perhaps twenty variously sized, grouped rocks—either a tight or a loose group—can be at the heart of a play space. They might be at the edge of a mound of dirt, near a low deck, or marking what will later be a planted area. Such a rock can later be sculpted with a drill and grinder to accommodate a waterfall and pool that will be a more permanent element of the landscape design.

When deciding how to group rocks, you will want to follow natural contours of the site where possible. Two-thirds of each large rock should be buried to prevent undesired movement and to make the rock look anchored in the earth. The rocks in a group should either be touching one another, or the spaces should be uneven, as shown in Fig. 11.1. As you contemplate a grouping-in-progress, you might be asking yourself whether the forms and textures you are exposing will be compatible with the theme or overall design plan of your garden.

Fig. 11.0

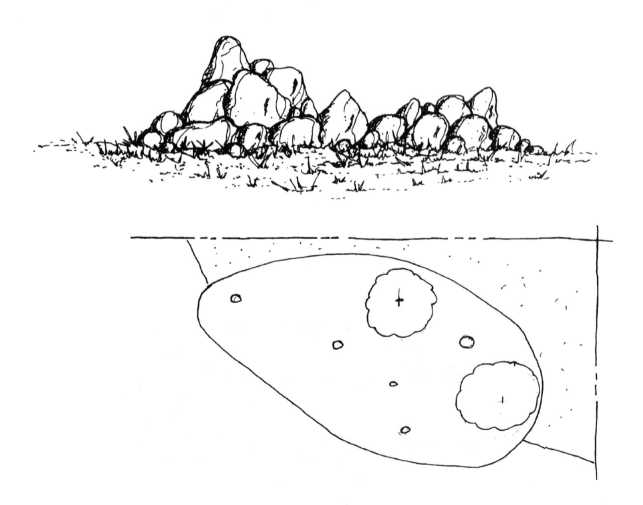

Fig. 11.1

Sand boxes. Sand is near the top of a list of all-time favorite places to play, for both boys and girls—sometimes lasting well into adulthood. It seems to stimulate imagination as few more elaborate playthings can do.

But sand needs to be contained in a landscape. A box, probably roofed to keep the sand dry, gives the young players a sense of security and even privacy, as fantasies direct their activity. Figure 11.2 shows a sandbox that can be covered by a section of deck made to slide over the box when it is not in use. The box shown in Figure 11.3 is the classic wooden square or rectangle. Although it appears here isolated from any other landscape feature, its size and placement need to be determined by the site. For example, it might be 4' x 4' and placed where a future annual or perennial bed will be. At that time, the sandbox becomes a raised bed, perhaps containing herbs or salad greens—a point of emphasis within the surrounding low-growing shrubs, ground cover, or hard-surfaced patio.

Hill-climb. A fairly large section of a landscape can be devoted to a hill (or mound) for climbing. Figures 11.4 and 11.5 show this idea in two views: the first an overall concept for location, the second a more detailed visualization. The mound rises perhaps five feet, with landscape timbers creating a maze-like route to the top. Planted with hardy grasses, its other immediate function is to prevent heavy runoff of rain (assuming a rainy climate).

Fig. 11.2

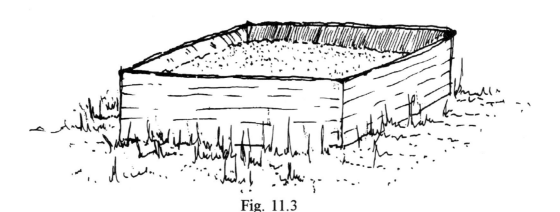

Fig. 11.3

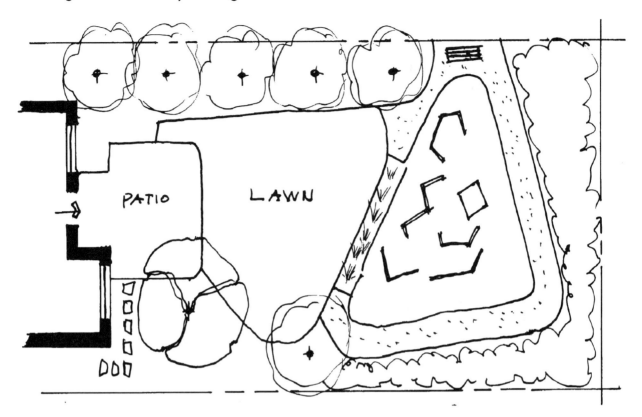

Fig. 11.4

Fig. 11.5

After the children have lost all interest in climbing such a puny hill, it stays intact but becomes a place for planting vegetables, flowers, or perhaps just vines. A pergola or bench at the top of the mound might be a place for adults to take the air or have a late-afternoon drink.

Pools. Plastic wading pools can seem more attractive and more fun if they are set into a specially designed area such as those suggested in the following three figures. Flat rocks build up the sides of the pool in Figure 11.6.

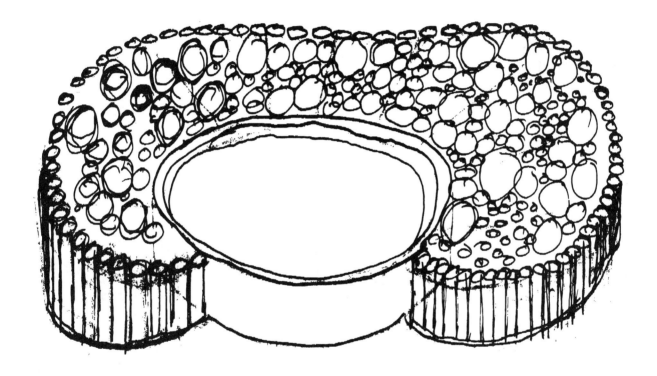

Fig. 11.6

In Figure 11.7, a dirt mound with steps places the pool two or three feet above the surrounding area. And in Figure 11.8, the pool is nestled among an array of rocks, grasses, and shrubs, giving it a slight aura of protection.

Fig. 11.7

Fig. 11.8

    Each of these kinds of pool settings can later be turned to another use or appearance. If standing water is no longer a desirable part of the design, the area can be filled in and planted to make a bog garden or other combination of plants, framed by what had been the pool sides.

   Upright logs. Treated logs or timbers (not creosoted railroad ties) of various lengths can be upended and placed in the earth to make inviting groupings, as Figures 11.9 and 11.10 suggest. Especially if the site has a slope that needs retaining or vertical definition, the logs can be placed with an eye to climbing and hide-and-seek fun, as well as to later use for planting. Spread out over a fairly wide area, they can become the background and accents for low, tough evergreens, grasses, or a few taller trees.

Fig. 11.9

Fig. 11.10

   Wire columns. Similar to the use of upright logs is a grouping of tall, circular wire columns. If they are sturdy enough and solidly placed in the ground, they are climbing poles, as Figure 11.11 shows, sprouting tall grasses even while they are climbable. The presence of such vegetation also makes the column area a good one for hide and seek.
   When those activities are done for good, the columns might be moved to an area devoted to vegetable growing or to other parts of the landscape as accent pieces or space dividers, with climbing, flowering vines covering them.

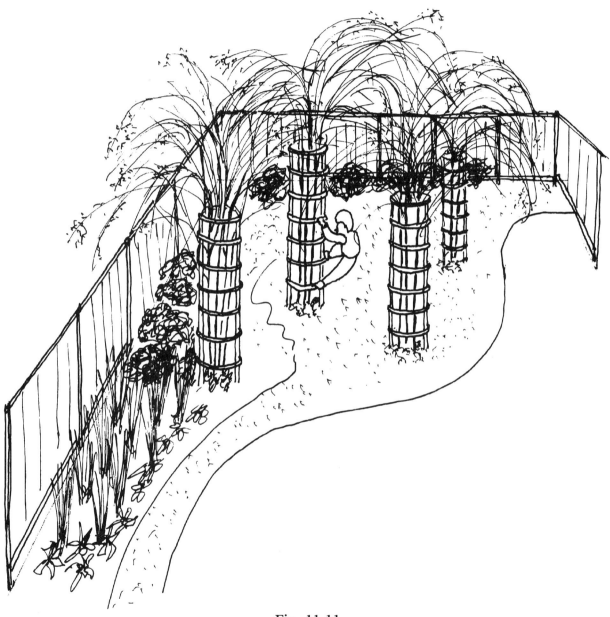

Fig. 11.11

Each of these ideas, we think, represents a desirable alternative to merely purchasing a ready-made swing set or other play equipment. They capitalize on materials that are more nearly part of the natural landscape, and they lower the chance of being stuck with an eyesore as disuse and rust take over.

Chapter 12

REMODELING A GARDEN

In Chapters 7, "Streetside Gardens and Entry Areas," and 8, "Sideyards and Corner Lots," we suggested that areas often not first thought of as suitable for gardens can be adapted to that purpose. More likely, many people think first of an expanse of backyard—one that is already level and has good soil—as the place to plant a garden, particularly if it will feature lettuce, radishes, and such. Nothing wrong with that, of course, but maybe garden ideas can be a little more ingenious to make a good-sized back yard multi-purpose.

A good way to determine how to use space is to sort through requirements and preferences, using the following checklist of questions:

• What kind of garden do you want—contemporary, natural or native, traditional, or period? Will this kind of garden harmonize with the house?

• What other main usage areas need to be accommodated along with the garden?

___ entry court
___ parking and/or turnaround
___ terrace/patio/deck
___ service
___ play
___ workspace
___ pool
___ other _____

A GLIMPSE AT DEFINITIONS

A <u>period garden</u> design is associated with a particular historical period, such as Victorian or Italian renaissance, or with a style, such as Williamsburg or English Cottage. The styles, of course, are usually closely related to an historical period. Many books are available in public libraries to guide you in recognizing the traits of each of these period designs.

The <u>traditional garden</u> also follows some precedent from the past but probably not quite so exactly or literally as the period design cited above. Because it was so commonly used in a region of a country, it simply became traditional by default. In the Pacific Northwest, for example, many gardens from the 1950's featured rolling lawns, trees and shrubs placed close to the house, and informal patios. The appearance of hundreds or thousands of such garden designs made them traditional—and therefore a powerful influence on people's ideas about the kind of garden they ought to have.

• What are your priority-ranked choices for types of plantings?

___ vegetables
___ flowers
___ shrubs
___ bulbs
___ fruit trees
___ ornamental trees
___ herbs
___ other _____

• How do you feel about intensity of maintenance?

___ willing to do a lot throughout the year
___ want minimal daily, seasonal, and annual chores

Contemporary designs are, by definition, in flux. They're whatever seems most popular at the moment. The availability of new materials, such as concrete pavers, helps determine the forms that contemporary designs may take. For many people, usefulness and ease of functioning are primary requisites of a contemporary garden.

The natural garden capitalizes on whatever materials and forms are present in Nature, such as earth, water, rock, and trees and shrubs in informal arrangements. When you see a natural garden, you might think it had occurred without human intervention, or, at any rate, that's what the designer hoped you would think. Indeed, the "natural" garden might have been skillfully contrived to imitate Nature though every part of it was carefully selected and placed by the designer. The plants used in a natural garden almost certainly are compatible with native species—no orchids in Minnesota!

A native garden comes closer than any of the preceding four types to being truly natural. It uses only indigenous materials and capitalizes on Nature's informal or random way of placing these materials. Because new plant materials come from reseeding or underground roots, they will appear as groves or masses. The designer simply makes path or trails through these masses, perhaps adding a few ornamental plants if they are entirely compatible with what is native to the area.

The way you answer these questions will importantly influence your conceptual plan. By referring to Chapter 16 on details of plants, you will be able to translate most of these specifications and preferences into detailed choices for execution. But right now, you need to be concerned about how to accommodate and integrate your overall preferences.

If you are dealing with a site that already has a garden—maybe one that has been there for twenty-five years and has become unruly or bedraggled—you can become a garden remodeler. Maybe the original owner had no concept of design and just plopped a few shrubs and trees in the most obvious places. Now you come along and realize that there were much better design principles that could have been used. It's time to correct old mistakes! This can be even more challenging and fun than starting from scratch.

Since you will probably want to rethink and redefine the uses of available space, you may be tempted to rip everything out and start fresh. Don't. At least not first thing. Instead, do this: identify every major tree and bush that's on the property. Do this either with plant-identification book in hand and pad at the ready, or take fresh branches (not a leaf or a twig) to a nursery worker, master gardener, or arboretum office. Find out not only the names of the existing plants but also their characteristics: evergreen or deciduous, root structure patterns (e.g., close to surface, widely travelling), eventual maximum height and spread. Keep this information in mind as you get closer to your detailed plan so that you can make an informed choice about which plants to chop and which to save.

At the conceptual stage, try to think of several of the existing trees or bushes that you like as a basis for the new design. Maybe they presently frame distant views, for example. Maybe they provide a pleasant screen from the street, particularly in summer, and should be preserved for that feature alone. By all means, don't think that a large, old evergreen has to come down just because it drops needles on the roof and in the gutters or because it provides a little too much shade. Such a tree has nobility, is probably far older than the humans who inhabit the place, and deserves veneration.

Also, you should step back from the site again to look at large plants in relation to front and back entries. If either is too heavily screened or seems to be surrounded by plants that don't make it both inviting and efficient to move through, you will want to design changes—from severe pruning to replacement.

Following are a few sketches that suggest some common problems with remodeled gardens—both before and approximate-after views.

In Figure 12.0, you see two or three common problems associated with an old patio or terrace:

— the free-form concrete surface is out of style (Kidney shapes were OK
    in the 50s, perhaps, but are generally no longer liked.)
— the concrete has settled and cracked in places and is therefore both
    unsightly and unsafe
— the patio form was never integrated into a more comprehensive
    design for the space.

Figure 12.1 shows a possible remodeling scheme. If we can be sure that no further settling is likely, we can place unit pavers on top of the concrete surface with mortar to produce interesting shapes and patterns. The remodeling scheme also shows how the pre-existing patio shape can be blended into a larger design, in this case expanding and building upon the initial shape.

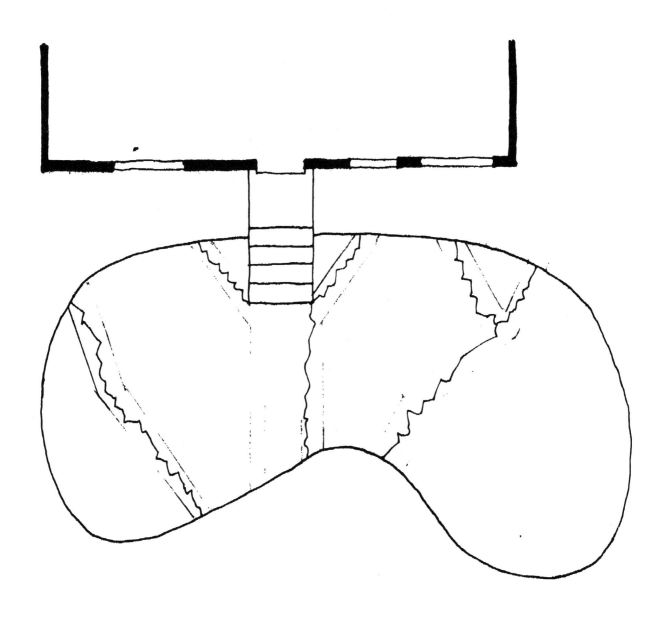

Fig. 12.0

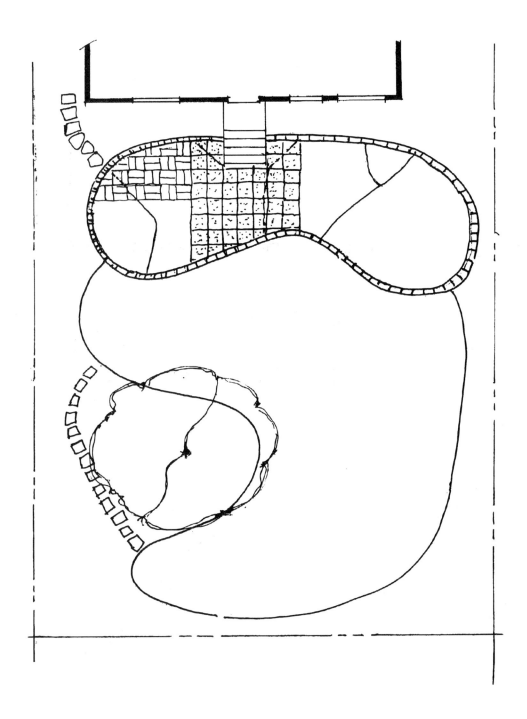

Fig. 12.1

The plantings shown in Figure 12.2 are characteristic of the tradition of 1920 and 1930. Several different plant forms placed in a nearly random manner clutter the design. Furthermore, since the trees and shrubs were probably not selected with an eye to their eventual size, they have become overgrown for the space—particularly the tree near the door. It must be removed and replaced by slow-growing edging plants and one deciduous shrub kept to a maximum height of four to five feet, as shown in Figure 12.3.

The other trees and bushes can be transplanted to clear the space for another use and to provide screening from the street. Transplanting of mature plants needs to occur over a period of about a year, starting with root pruning, trenching, and backfilling with compost. Later, "balling" the plant and moving it to a new position will assure a successful transplant.

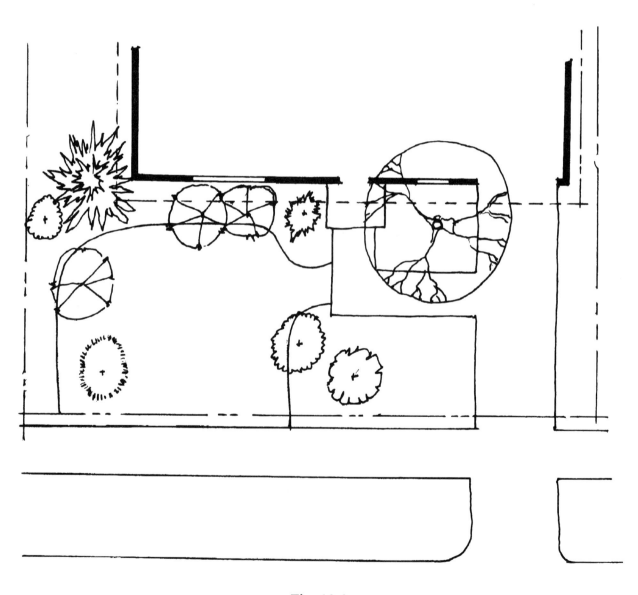

Fig. 12.2

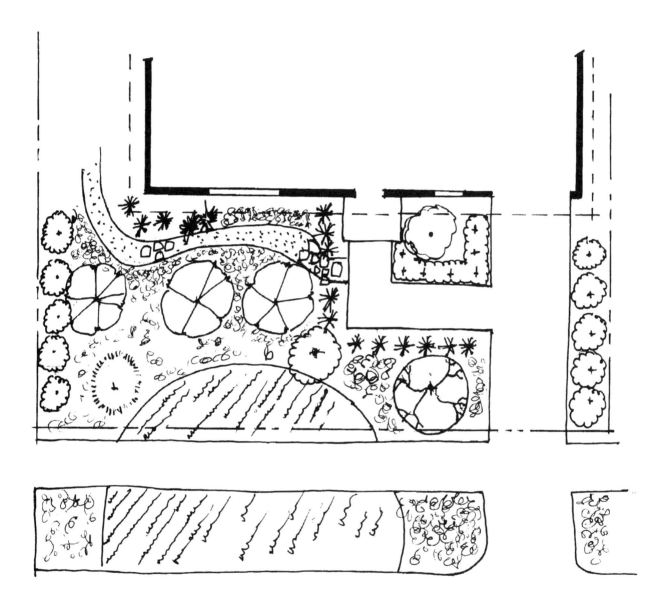

Fig. 12.3

Another typical design from the 1920s is shown in Figure 12.4: the long driveway next to the house, approaching a detached garage. The effect is tunnel-like, the space seemingly usable for only the single purpose.

Figure 12.5 suggests that the old driveway can become an entry walk by adding unit pavers to both sides of the car tracks (especially if the garage is no longer to be used for car storage). If the concrete car tracks have become cracked, they can be broken into smaller pieces and re-laid, interspersed with hardy ground cover.

These are just a few of the common situations that lead to ideas about remodeling a landscape. Any garden may seem to need remodeling, depending upon the styles popular at the time and upon a new owner's needs and preferences. Since this book has led you through a process of critiquing a site—both its existing design features and its potential for change—you will, of course, draw on other ideas for remodeling, such as we have proposed in Chapters 5 through 10.

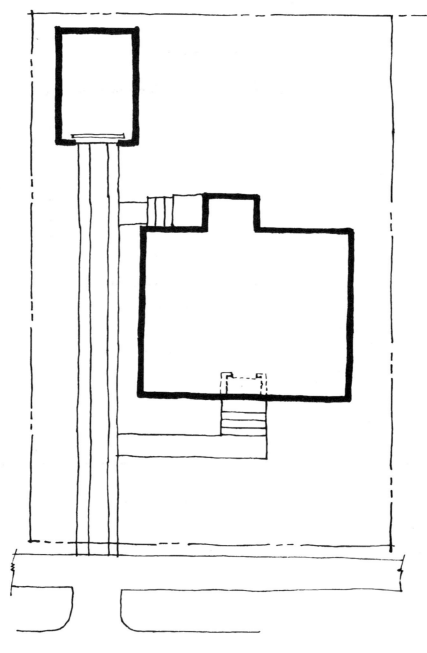

Fig. 12.4

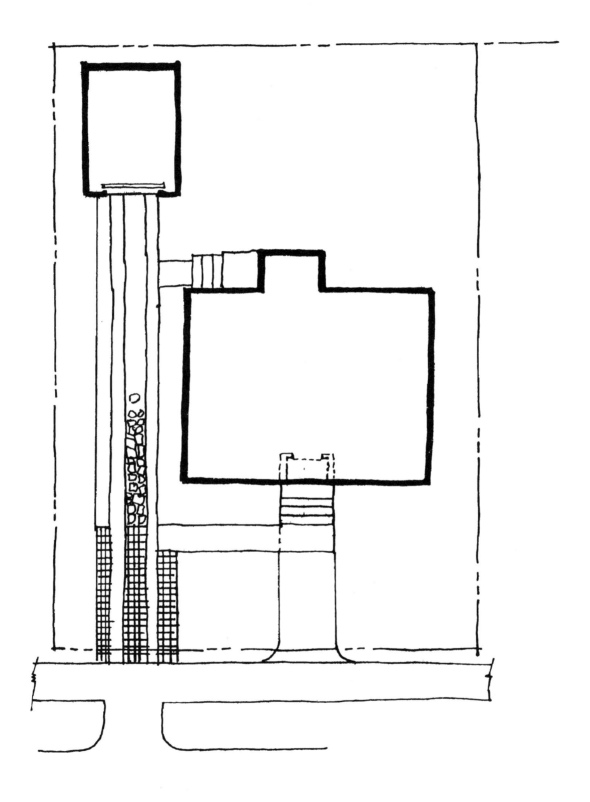

Fig. 12.5

Chapter 13

OBSERVING AND CRITIQUING GARDENS

As you have been thinking about what really needs to be in your landscape design and how it will best suit your needs, you may find it helpful to look elsewhere for a while. That is, before you narrow too much your self-generated ideas for a design, you should probably take a close look at what others have done. Ideas for gardens aren't copyrighted. Maybe somebody else's solution to a landscape problem will be similar to what you should do.

We suggest, first, that you do some intensive observing, both of actual gardens and of photographs. Take a few notes. Snap a few pictures of your own to bolster your memories of what you've seen.

Second, use the evaluation checklist on p.130 to help formulate your preferences and summarize your choices.

LOOKING AT PHOTOGRAPHS

In the magazine back-issues section of your local library, get copies of several garden magazines (such as, *Better Homes and Gardens, Sunset, Pacific Horticulture, Horticulture*). Examine photographs for these design elements:

Patios, terraces, and decks. Look at the size of the area, the construction materials, details, circulation patterns, focal points (such as, steps, benches, planters, pots, colors, textures). Notice how plants surround the area of the tree canopy. While you're at it, see if the photographs are accompanied by sectional drawings and details about how to make these structures.

Features. Study such garden features as pools, waterfalls, sculpture, and rock formations with plants.

Plantings. Note the locations of major plants and how they occur at focal or accent points. Also, take note of the plant forms or masses and how they separate spaces. Then, look at individual plants (later, looking up information on which USDA climate zones they grow in). Finally, bring to conscious attention the design principles illustrated in these plantings: how is variety achieved through textural contrast? are all the plantings in harmony with one another?

STUDYING PROFESSIONAL LANDSCAPE DESIGNS

Most urban environments have landscape designs that have been created by professionals. They might include an in-city, "pocket" park or a courtyard for a major office building. Because they had to be created to fit tight restrictions, they probably reflect long, careful thought about how to make the best use of space. It will be well worth your time to view such a built landscape from all angles. Use your design-alert eyes to consider such qualities as these:

- Does the landscape design seem to blend or tie visually with nearby structures (such as office buildings, streets, bus stops)?
- How does the design invite passersby to look and/or linger (e.g., with such a feature as a fountain or a waterfall, use of interesting rock or textured surfaces, pathways and sitting places that say "Come in")?
- Are the plant materials "ordinary," that is, without surprise or distinctiveness? or unsuitably exotic? or distinctive but not bizarre?
- What appear to be the maintenance requirements?
- How has lighting—both natural and artificial—been used to enhance the textures and arrangements of plants and building materials?

You may want to aid your memory of these observations by taking a few snapshots of this professional design—whether or not you think it succeeds. You might also take out your sketchbook and rattle off a few quick sketches from a couple of viewing perspectives. A few notes about textures or plant characteristics might also be useful.

DRIVING OR WALKING AROUND NEIGHBORHOODS

In our usual driving, most of us don't really look at the environment with conscious attention. We move through it, paying attention only to where we're going and becoming habituated to what we see. When we change our perspective from looking **through** to looking **at**, we discover a lot that we've missed.

So, on a weekend, during early morning or late afternoon—anytime when you don't have to get from here to there at a certain time—wander through one or more neighborhoods: fancy ones, ordinary ones, even rundown ones. You want a wide range of landscape-seeing experiences: attractive ones heightened or made more instructive through contrast with those that are unattractive.

Houses. Are they nestled into their surroundings—looking as though house and site were conceived as an integrated composition? Do the plants make the houses look larger than they might without the plants? Or are the plants so large that they seem to dwarf the house?

If a house has picture windows, do the plants hide the view? Pretend that you are in the house, looking out. Do the plantings enclose the front area, probably giving a comfortable sense of boundaries without enclosing the house like a fortress?

As you see characteristics of houses that are similar to the house you're working with, can you sort out a few ideas for plantings that might work for you?

Entries to houses. Can you spot the entry to each house easily? Would a visitor be confused about where to find the door? Are the entries to scale and inviting? If so, how was that highly desirable trait achieved?

Where are driveways and parking areas located in relation to the house? Will their locations make access easy? In relation to the front door, is there room enough to park a car, not too far away, and to turn the car around or back into the street? What's your overall sense of each entry: welcoming/forbidding, graceful/tasteless, planned/haphazard, convenient/awkward?

Steps. If any steps are involved in approaching doors, decks, or other structures, are they wide enough (i.e., room for two people to walk side-by-side)? Do they look inviting (secure and solid, not slippery)?

Are the walks leading to the steps wide enough and made of materials that harmonize with the house materials?

Do any plantings along the walks lead one to the front door? Are they the type that will rapidly encroach, as they grow, on normal walking along the path?

Do entry areas lead to any surprises—turns in the walkway, views of plantings or garden features—that make the approach to the door more intriguing? Do you have the feeling, as you view an entry court from the street, that you'd really like to peek inside, whether or not your mission is to visit the people who live there?

Maintenance. As you're looking at each house and entry, consider the maintenance involved in the design. What will it take—in the way of raking, pruning, cultivating, replacing plants and other materials—to keep the place looking good?

Problems. Particularly with landscaping that is twenty-five or more years old, you are likely to notice some problems that have developed. A principal problem is overgrowth: plants that have gone untended so they have formed a jungle and the house has been obscured. (If the house has gone similarly untended, perhaps the jungle is a minor blessing, but in that case we're talking Gross Neglect.)

Another problem is a planting that has not so much outgrown the available space as its usefulness or functionality. (Maybe the plants hide a view or create a lopsided, disorienting effect because they grew at uneven rates.)

A third negative may be more a matter of preference than a bad physical problem, but notice the house that was planted with vertical shrubs at the corners of the house. Don't they emphasize the height of the house rather than its horizontal base on the site? And don't most human activities orient themselves to the horizontal plane? Then why not select a planting design that is likely to accommodate that fact?

EVALUATING YOUR OBSERVATIONS

While your handwritten notes and sketches, plus any photos you take, will help a lot in your remembering what you liked and didn't like on your wanderings, you'll probably be glad you formalized your observations a little more. You can use the evaluation form (page 130) as a means for "scoring" each garden. (We hate the idea of simplistically grading a landscape design, but we suggest only a rough and tentative screening of your preferences along a fairly stable scale.)

We've supplied abbreviated statements of criteria or standards, with a scoring scale following each criterion statement. In the spaces across the top, write in the addresses of the houses and gardens you observe. As you complete your observation of each site, circle the number below each criterion that best expresses your evaluation. It doesn't matter whether you add up the total because all you really need is a numeric reminder of the features of each garden that you liked best and may want to incorporate in your own design.

STANDARDS FOR EVALUATING LANDSCAPE DESIGN

The best garden is one full of useful, enjoyable spaces for people, unified with plants and/or combined with constructed elements. The house should be an integral part of the garden (i.e., unified by function, style, materials, rooms, doors, walks).

Address of house: _____

_____

Directions: Using 10 as high and 1 as low, rate each house and garden by each criterion.

I First impression of the garden

      1   2   3   4   5   6   7   8   9   10

II Purpose of the garden (e.g., passive, useful, sculptural, edible, traditional)

      1   2   3   4   5   6   7   8   9   10

III Design—functional aspect

Is the garden functional for the purpose?

      1   2   3   4   5   6   7   8   9   10

Is the entrance easy to find and inviting?

      1   2   3   4   5   6   7   8   9   10

Design—aesthetic aspect

Were principles of balance, rhythm, emphasis, scale, and proportion followed?

      1   2   3   4   5   6   7   8   9   10

Were elements of design (i.e., line, form, pattern, texture, color) followed?

      1   2   3   4   5   6   7   8   9   10

IV Construction of garden

Are the constructed elements (i.e., paved areas, decking, walls, fences, pools, benches, etc.) well-constructed and maintained?

      1   2   3   4   5   6   7   8   9   10

V Plant materials

Are the plants (i.e., trees, shrubs) in scale with the house?

      1   2   3   4   5   6   7   8   9   10

Is the choice of plants suited to the site (e.g., to define spaces, give privacy)?

      1   2   3   4   5   6   7   8   9   10

Are plants chosen for correct function, exposure (i.e., sun/shade), soils, drainage, etc.?

      1   2   3   4   5   6   7   8   9   10

Are the plants healthy and maintained?

      1   2   3   4   5   6   7   8   9   10

VI Final impression

Would you want to come back to see this garden at another time of day or season?

      1   2   3   4   5   6   7   8   9   10

Chapter 14

FROM CONCEPTUAL PLAN TO ALMOST-FINAL PLAN

As you have read the last seven chapters, you have probably imagined the several parts of your conceptual plan more specifically. One possible element—such as a deck or a large tree to be preserved—triggers thoughts about another element and how they will fit together. In fact, you may be feeling overwhelmed with details, to the point that you feel as though proper landscaping is just too complicated for an amateur.

If you do feel that way, be glad! It probably means that you are reaching the point of fullness—of ideas. You are ready, we hope, to start committing yourself to decisions. It may also mean that you are beyond the point of naively believing that designing a garden well requires little more than an afternoon's visit to a nursery.

So, you're ready to proceed from the conceptual plans you spawned (see Chapter 6) to one that is—can we say it?— final. "Almost-final"? We don't want to suggest certainty here, because "final" plans more often than not turn out to anything but final. Revision is always possible, depending upon available time and size of budget. Big changes after work has begun on the ground can prove costly if large objects, extensive grading, walls, and so forth are involved. On the other hand, many smaller choices can't be made until you see the actual placements and relationships of elements. The plan you create on paper at this stage, then, is intended to represent fairly definite choices, with fairly specific details about what goes where.

With just a few (probably no more than half a dozen) of the sheets containing the conceptual plans (from Chapter 6) you like best in front of you, get out another sheet of tracing paper and tack it to your drawing surface. Mark in the house footprint and lot outline, and sit with your soft-leaded pencil at the ready. Don't get tense, but do pause to appreciate the grandeur of the moment. You're about to translate a concept—a vague or fuzzy conglomeration of images—into a representation of a future reality. You should have a feeling of power, of adventure, of kinship with Mother Nature, that Great Designer of Us All!

Draw the footprint of the house and any existing structures such as a garage. Then, as we illustrate in Fig. 14.0, extend the lines of the house to the property lines on all sides. These lines include all walls, windows, and doors. The purpose of this line-extending step is to start defining large outdoor areas, enabling you to locate to best advantage pathways, main garden elements (such as patios), fences, screens, and trellises. In effect, you are using the inside areas of the house—and the views from them to outside—to define outdoor spaces.

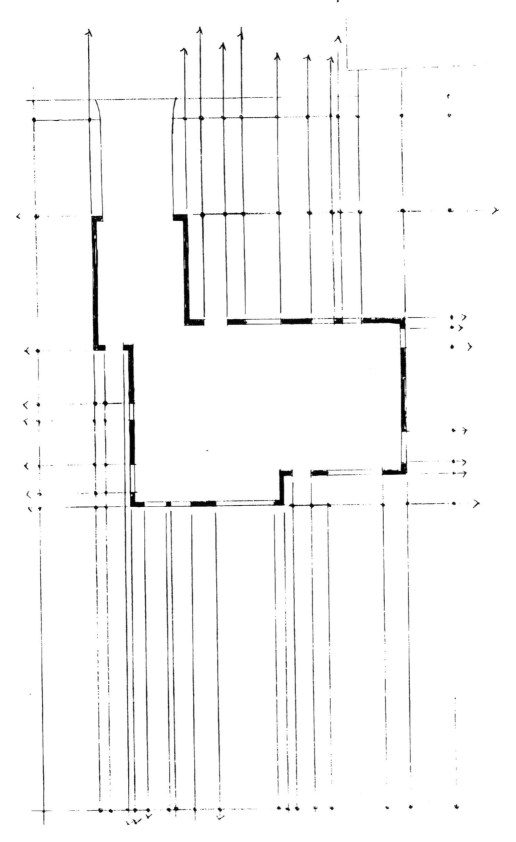

Fig. 14.0

This done, proceed as we show in Fig. 14.1 to outline the shapes that are potentially defined by the window extension lines. Notice that the angular lines marking the width of each shape are determined by an imaginary inside viewer, who is standing one or two feet from each window. Do you see now why this method is called "visual angular method of design"?

Now sketch—as near to scale as possible—the top-view outlines of to-be-built structures, like decks, terraces, walls, and fences, locating them plausibly in relation to the shapes you have just drawn. Whether one choice is more plausible than another depends upon 1) the expected function (as of a deck or a screening fence), 2) climate-control considerations, and 3) hoped-for appeal to the eye. What you should be trying for is the best possible integration of the needs and desires you listed in Chapter 2.

Then, using small crosses for bushes, shrubs, and smaller plants (such as groundcover) and circles for trees, mark the places that suit each of these plantings. You may not have the name of each type of tree or plant in mind, but you should have at least an image of how each one might look. Probable height and width, proportional relationships of one to another, and density of coverage will be among the components of that image. Chapter 16 will help you become more specific about each of these plant options.

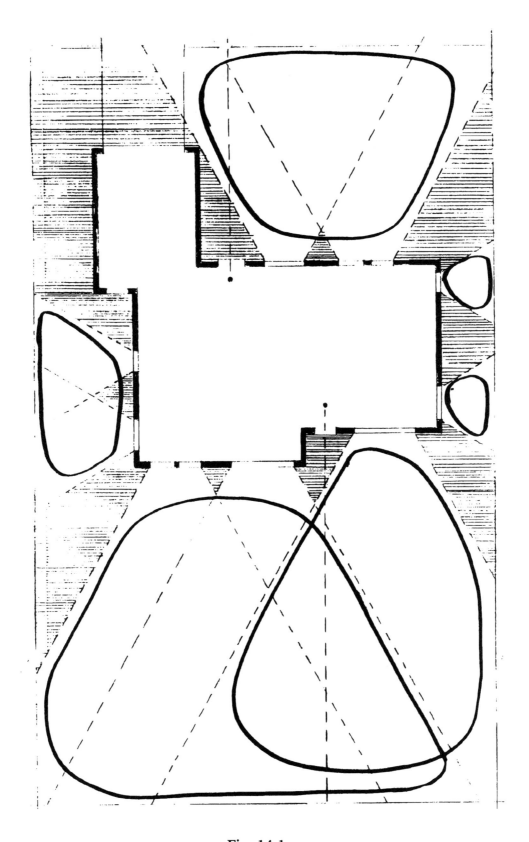

Fig. 14.1

Following is an example (Fig. 14.2) of how one garden designer moved from conceptual plan to "final" plan. We have included a letter-key for this designer's final plan simply to guide you in connecting plan decisions with the owner's needs and desires.

A = an entry court. The owner wanted a "sense of entry," as professional designers say—a space that is clearly marked as a transition between street and house. Such a court encourages visitors to adjust their perceptions as they move from a space requiring a "public" attitude to one where a more private one is appropriate.

B = two patios—upper and lower. They are intended both for entertaining and for interesting views of plant textures and paving patterns as seen from kitchen nook, dining room, and living room.

C = low-growing vegetation, providing color and texture year-round

D1 = coniferous tree to frame a distant view and separate spaces

D2 = small trees in parking strip to provide screening

D3 = small, slow-growing tree to provide accent (an interesting visual feature)

E = wood fences—just high enough to provide privacy from neighbors and passersby and not connected to one another, adding visual interest and a better sense of space integration

F = rock walls softened with vines and spreading vegetation

G = small lawn. The owner plans to use it occasionally as a putting green.

H = patch of grass in parking strip—a bow to the widely held view that some grass is necessary in a parking strip

I = groundcover in parking strip. This treatment provides minimum maintenance, especially if the site is on a hill.

J = evergreens of mixed varieties and sizes. They provide a screening border and visual interest.

K = small pool. The owners want this to be a visual and aural feature to arouse a sense of surprise and delight.

L = narrow side yard access to lower patio and grass area—a woodland pathway

M = mini-private space to be enjoyed by guests at front door

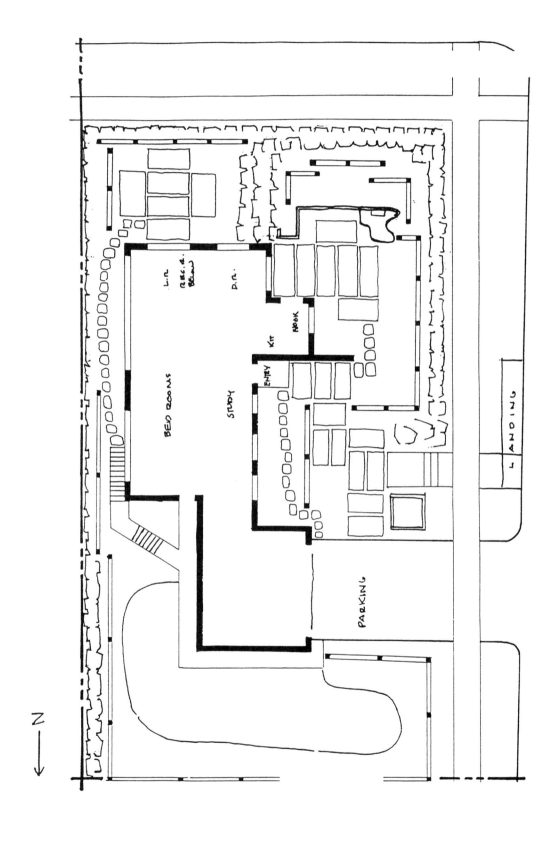

Fig. 14.2

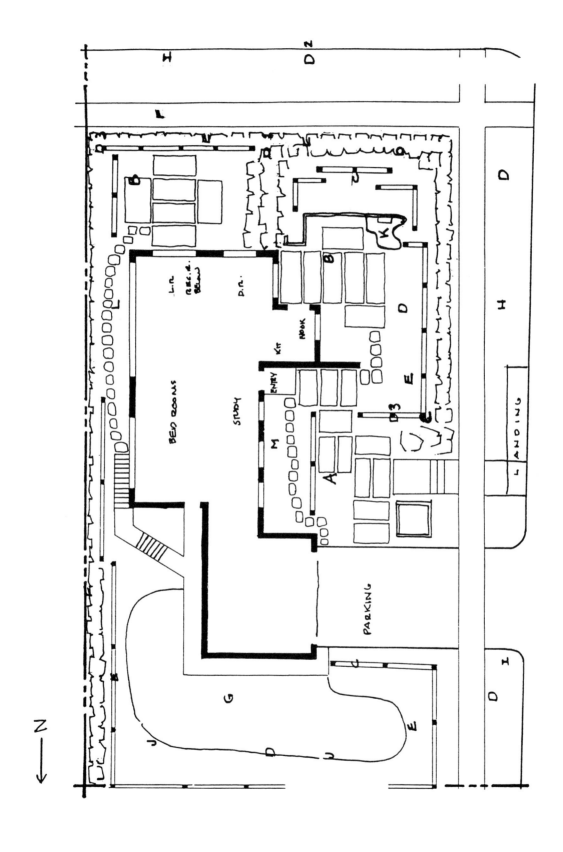

Fig. 14.2 with Letter-Key for Choices in Sample Final Plan

Because the making of a final plan involves specifics of plants and other landscaping materials, you obviously need greater amounts of particular knowledge about what's available and possible. We can't make recommendations for these specifics, because regional climates and all the other idiosyncrasies of a site and an owner must first be known. But we do ask you to consider a few additional questions as you narrow down the choices.

Question #1: What materials are going to be underfoot—your feet, if you occupy the property, and the feet of guests and other visitors? If you've decided to have a deck, with steps leading to the ground, will you alight on a hard or a soft surface? If hard, you'll need to consider ease of installation, cost, and maintenance. (See Appendix B, page 173 for a list of possible surfacing materials, with accompanying details.) If soft, such as a seeded lawn, you'll want to think ahead toward watering, mowing, and fertilizing—all those high-intensity maintenance jobs that never end.

Question #2: What materials are going to be around you—to separate the spaces you have planned and to provide privacy? Think about walking or sitting in various parts of the space, and then try to visualize the textures you want to see: a vine-covered trellis surrounding a sitting area; a solid wood screen that repeats materials and colors used in the house exterior, again for hiding unpleasant views or for privacy; clumps of cascading bushes, or a tall tree with breathing space around it, or carefully- ineated areas for certain varieties of flowers or vegetables.

Question #3: What, if anything, will be between the top of your head and the open sky? Will you need protection from the sun? Or from the gaze of near or distant neighbors, whose views from higher sites include everything you and others do when you are outside? Some sort of canopy—whether of built materials or living ones—may be welcome as you make full use of your newly-designed outdoor space.

As you form your answers to these questions, try to think in more than two dimensions. Your on-paper version of the plan, of course, exists only two-dimensionally. But you're going to develop it in three dimensions. And there will even be a fourth dimension to think about—time—because living things are not static. Everything changes, so you need to try to imagine the growth of plants especially. They will cast shadows, drop leaves or needles, become bushier or spindlier, mask areas presently open to view. You can't do this with stunning clarity and exactness, but you can anticipate some of the main kinds of inevitable change. In Chapter 16, we present more detail on choices of specific plants to use in a planting design.

Before you examine those details, though, we suggest the option of making a model of your proposed plan (Chapter 15). It's one excellent way of assisting you in three-dimensional thought.

Chapter 15

MAKING A THREE-DIMENSIONAL
STUDY MODEL

Isn't it terribly difficult to make a scale model, complete with land contours, building(s), and landscaping? Don't you have to have excellent craft skills, a lot of time, and maybe quite a bit of money? The answer to these questions is no.

But even if almost anyone can cheaply make a useful model, why should you? Especially if you are working with a site that is close at hand—so you can see everything about it easily—what will a model show you that you might need or value?

We'd like to persuade you that a simple cardboard model—set in a sandbox that imitates in miniature the lot you're working with—can help you greatly in visualizing the landscaped look you want to achieve. Visualizing it in advance of any actual on-site work can save you time and money, and it may even stimulate your imagination still further as to the best combination of elements. We suggest that this is true for any landscape project. One that involves a hillside, however, may actually <u>demand</u> a model if serious miscalculations are to be avoided.

We urge you to read the explanation that follows with a receptive attitude.

STEPS IN MODEL-MAKING

Since a useful model needs to be built to scale, you're going to need accurate measurements to start. From your previous measuring, you may already have the dimensions of the lot and the buildings. If not, or if you are working with a hillside lot, you may need the assistance of a civil engineer to make a contour map of the property. (The Yellow Pages can lead you to such a person.) Or, if you want to take your own elevations (i.e., make the measurements of a hilly lot), you may use one of the methods illustrated in this book (Chapter 4). It will be a good idea to practice the measurement methods before proceeding on your own landscape. Accuracy is very important.

<u>Scale</u>. Once you have accurate measurements of every major part of your lot and buildings, decide on a scale for the model. We suggest either 1/8" or 1/4" on the model for each foot of actual measurement.

<u>Materials</u>. Start with a sheet for showing contour lines and one for the building or buildings (including any new construction that may be part of your project, such as a garage, a deck,

or other outbuilding).   Tagboard or other stiff cardboard (e.g., 11" x 17"), preferably white, works well for these purposes.   You'll will also need thin (1/8") plywood and/or pieces of soft wood like pine or fir, sand, and duct tape for making a box. Materials you'll need later include simulated trees and other plant materials, and perhaps stones or certain inorganic stuff. See Photograph 15.0.

    <u>Tools</u>. A sharp-bladed knife, scissors, a wood saw, a ruler, glue, and transparent tape are probably the only tools you'll need. You may want to use colored pencils or crayons for heightening the realism of the model.

    <u>Drawing, cutting and assembly</u>. Using a soft pencil, draw in outline all the components you need to represent structures—separate pieces for the floor plan, each side of the house, and any other box-like structures. Draw as many sides as you can continuously on one sheet of tagboard, so that, after folding, you will have a more rigid building form. Remember to stick to your scale measurements so that everything will fit together well.

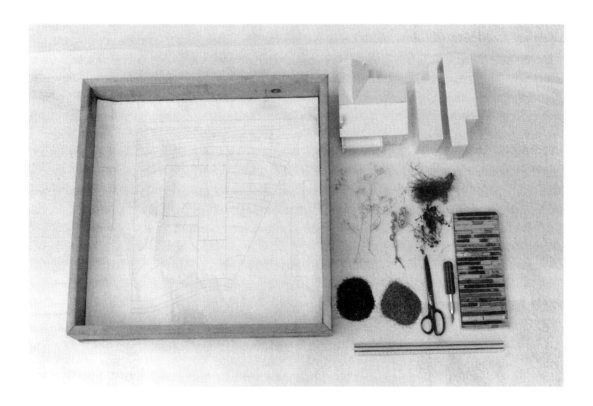

Photograph 15.0

Draw the outlines of all doors and windows. Whether you include roofs is up to you. They aren't really necessary for the model, though, of course, including them will give you a more realistic representation. Cut out the pieces with a sharp-bladed knife so that edges are clean. Fasten them together either with transparent tape or with tagboard L's (small rectangular strips folded in the middle to create a right angle) glued on the inside of the model.

SITUATING THE MODEL

When you have assembled the models of all pertinent structures, you need to situate them in a simulated environment. Just placing these models on a table, after all, isn't going to give you much of a feeling about how the structures fit into a landscaped setting.

So, we recommend that you next create a plywood sandbox that simulates your lot. If it's a steeply sloping lot, the box needs to reflect that slope to scale—with highest and lowest sides clearly modelled in the box shape. Cut a bottom piece that exactly reflects the perimeter of the lot, probably using plywood or something similar (not cardboard), and side pieces to match the contour of the lot. If the lot is not steeply sloping, a box with matching sides will be OK. (See Photograph 15.0.) In either case, a sheet cut to fit the inside of the box will indicate building footprint(s) and contour lines.

Fasten the side pieces to the bottom with duct tape or some other material that will adequately contain the wet sand that you are going to pour in.

Coarse grey sand that you can get from a building materials store will work fine to provide a simulation of the earth your building sits on and out of which your landscaping dreams will rise. Wet the sand first so that you can shape it to match the approximate contour of the lot you're dealing with. (Clay or plaster of Paris can also be used, but they're both more expensive and somewhat harder to work with. Clay, however, has the advantage of holding upright your simulated walls and trees and may, in fact, be necessary for simulating a steeply sloping lot. See Photograph 15.1.)

Photograph 15.1

After you've shaped the sand to represent the site contours, place the building models, measuring from the side of the box to locate them accurately. See Photograph 15.2.

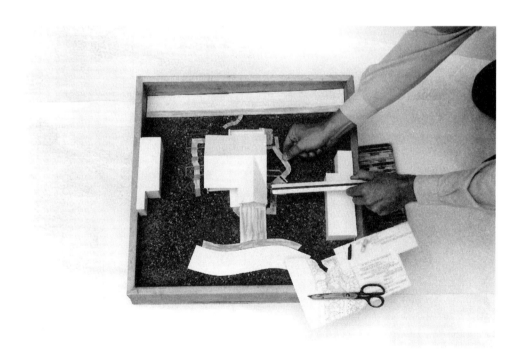

Photograph 15.2

ADORNING THE MODEL

Now that the building(s) and the immediate surface features are represented and in place, you're ready to fill in the proposed landscaping features—still to scale, of course. Here's a list of suggested materials for representing these adornments:

> trees: live twigs (snipped to represent desired shapes)
> bushes: wire or plastic mesh (shaped to represent masses,
>   not individual plants)
> grass: artificial turf (cut to suitable shape)
> fencing: balsa wood or cardboard painted to imitate wood
> walkways: painted cardboard (cut to suitable shape)

You should try to place all of these landscaping elements to correspond to the almost-final plan you've made. Before you fasten any of them down tightly, move them around a bit. Stand back from the model and look at them in relation to one another. Look at them from all sides, from above, and from various angles (maybe sometimes with one eye shut or with different sources and intensities of light). You might even photograph the model from different angles. Try to imagine yourself inside the house, looking out, or sitting on a porch or deck, looking at and then beyond the elements you're considering. Deliberating in these ways will probably heighten your sense of how your plan is actually going to function and how well it pleases you. (See Photographs 15.3 and 15.4.)

Photograph 15.3

Photograph 15.4

If this kind of in-the-round activity doesn't make you feel much more confident of the soundness (or lack of it) of your plan, we'll be greatly surprised. We suggest, too, that the usefulness of the model doesn't end once your landscaping is actually under way. Stored in a game room, garage, or classroom, the model will become a valuable part of any future scheme for planting or garden remodeling. It'll also make a great conversation piece for visitors who might be curious about your ideas.

Chapter 16

MAKING A PLANTING DESIGN

The design work you've done so far has helped you create a concept of the larger elements. You know where driveways and walkways will go; where you may want trees and groupings of bushes; where fences, walls, or trellises may be. The three-dimensional model has aided you in visualizing spatial relationships and maybe the effects of certain textures—heavy for screening, lighter for marking informal boundaries or creating pleasing variety.

But before you actually start buying or transplanting plants and putting them in the ground, you need more specific ideas for a planting design. We define that as the <u>combination of large and small plant materials chosen and placed to suit the basic circulation plan, built structures, topography, climate, and inhabitants' needs and carefully considered desires</u>. In making the planting design, you are rigorously narrowing down the possibilities for choice—making the decisions, based on preference and cost, that will finally determine your actual landscape.

Realize that you have a bewildering variety of specific plant choices that will likely work at your site. (See Figure 16.0.) In order to begin to reduce bewilderment and make workable choices, you have to study individual characteristics of plants: their heights in 10 years, their spread and rate of growth, root systems (shallow or deep), form, flowers, preferred sun exposure, water and soil requirements.

Fig. 16.0

You may find that you can move most efficiently toward your own planting design by making columns on several sheets, with the names of possible plant choices on the left and then a series of columns with each of the criteria listed in the preceding paragraph. See Appendix A, Plant Varieties and Characteristics, for a fairly complete listing of most relevant plant traits. Your priority list of traits may well be shorter; on the other hand, you may decide to use all or most of the characteristics shown in the twelve columns adjacent to the plant names.

Or, if one or more of these traits seems most important to you, your list might place that trait first, with names of plants that have that trait, like this:

EXAMPLE	
Sun exposure	Plant names
full	lavender compact strawberry bush
partial	mountain laurel winter daphne

We'll guide you through a series of steps that will enable you to do this narrowing down with some confidence.

Forms. Your "final" plan and model have pretty well established what basic shapes of plant materials will suit your site. We hope you have thought of these shapes as forms: the silhouette or outline of the plant (or plant mass, if they're clumps of bushes). At this stage, it's much more important to think first about the forms, rather than details like color of flowers or leaf shape. (See "Texture" below for that aspect of the planting design.)

Following are sketches that provide simple terms for the probable forms you've selected:

SHRUB FORMS

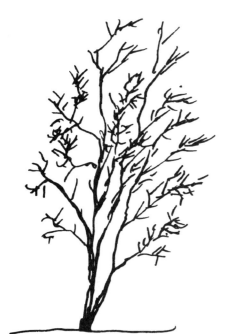

Clump
Figure 16.1

Low
Figure 16.2

TREE FORMS

Globe
Figure 16.3

Picturesque
Figure 16.4

Columnar
Figure 16.5

Weeping
Figure 16.6

In Appendix A, we have listed several specific names and characteristics of plant materials for each of these form categories. Attention must be paid to these characteristics if you are to make choices you won't later regret. Surely you would agree, for example, that a tree that has a lovely texture and size for a certain spot in your design but that can't stand temperatures below freezing won't do if you live in the same climate zone as Minnesota. Obvious? Yes, but surprisingly easy to forget.

Scale. Knowledge of the mature size of a specific tree or bush must be a part of any initial planting design. The immature plant you see in a nursery that looks just right for a certain spot may turn out to be hideously out of scale five years later. You must check on the projected mature size of any tree or bush you choose before you decide on using it.

One convenient way of checking is to ask employees at a nursery near you. Most nursery people are very knowledgeable about plants, since their livelihoods depend on that knowledge. You might bring your list of tentative choices to such a person and make notes about what s/he says on traits such as growth rate, water and soil requirements, and ability to tolerate sun. Furthermore, you're likely to find yourself getting even more interested in plants and respectful of their role in Nature. We can all benefit from heightening that awareness.

Texture. No doubt you have observed that plants differ in the density of their leaf outcroppings. Maple trees, for example, produce leaves luxuriantly, providing an almost complete screen between a viewer and an object beyond. Certain bushes—like burning bushes, some spireas and viburnums, and aromatic sumac—provide a tracery: leaves small and delicate, branches visible, a feathery screen mostly open to view. In choosing the right variety, you'll want to think about the amount of see-through you want—just how dense you want the plant mass to look. (Periodic pruning can, of course, help achieve this effect.)

An aspect of texture is the total number of plants placed in a given landscaped area. We have found that enthusiastic beginner landscapers tend to overdo it: they plant too many of everything. Besides adding unnecessarily to the cost, this exuberance results in a jumbled, overcrowded look. Remember the principle: less is more. Fewer carefully chosen and carefully spaced plants will achieve a superior lasting appearance.

We think the best choice is to plant any given variety in masses, rather than alternating varieties. Another mass or two of that same variety or species can be placed nearby, with either nothing or some contrasting variety in between.

Color. Will you want year-round green? Does it matter to you that all the leaves will fall off (and have to be raked up), while the plant enters its dormant season? Do you have a strong desire for the spring and early-summer reds, pinks, and whites of rhododendrons? the even-earlier red, pinks, and whites of camellias? the mid-fall look of gold, red, and yellow deciduous leaves?

Along with any thoughts you may have about the color of annual or perennial flowers—like nasturtium, rose, or ageratum—you'll want to try to get a sense of the balance of both stable and changing colors as your garden goes through its seasonal cycles. The planting design needs to reflect that sense. It would be a good idea here to recall the principles of design we introduced in Chapter 3. Try to think about combinations of plant materials that reflect principles of repetition, sequence, variety, and balance. Doing this while looking at your three-dimensional model will probably be a lot more feasible than trying to do it with unaided imagination.

A SAMPLE PLANTING DESIGN

To show how you might make the systematic choices of specific plant materials a part of your emerging plan, we present a sample planting design (Figure 16.7). The numbers refer to the type of plant chosen for each location. To study the reasons for each choice, you should consult Appendix A, where the characteristics of these choices are given in detail. However, we can summarize the owner's desires:

- several outdoor areas integrated with interior spaces ("so the outside will seem to be an extension of the inside")
- lots of privacy
- places to grow flowers so that "we will have color and texture year round, using woodland plants, perennials, and bulbs."

Two additional features of this planting design are not indicated, though they were among the owner's desires: a drip irrigation system and a low-voltage lighting system. They contribute both to the ease of proper plant maintenance and to heightening their visual appeal after sundown.

Notice that all the elements in this planting design are very simply drawn. A hedge is simply a zigzag line; shrub masses are shown by an undulating series of curves and plant centers, finally connecting to enclose an area; flower beds are a variation on the shrub outline; trees are circles drawn to suggest the type of tree, deciduous or evergreen.

In doing your planting design, you might want to try the overlay method—placing your proposed design over your plot plan. Either sheets of plastic or tracing paper will work.

By making several overlays, you'll be able to try out and judge several possible planting designs. Unless you follow a procedure such as this, you're likely to follow whims instead—buying whatever takes your fancy in a garden store or buying whatever your credit card allows at a given time. Whim-acquisition of plants negates design. Since we want you to create a landscape design that provides long-lasting satisfaction, we urge you to suppress your whims and not let the temporary and immediate appeal of pretty flowers or attractive foliage overwhelm your carefully worked-out design ideas.

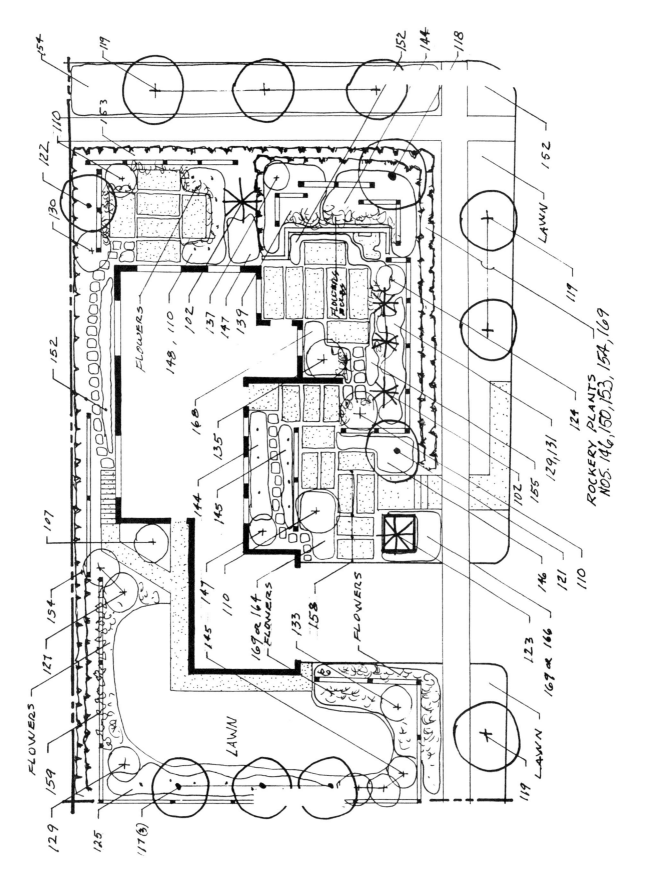

Fig. 16.7

NAMES OF PLANTS CORRESPONDING TO NUMBERS ON FIGURE 16.7

Trees

102	Scotch pine
117	snowdrop tree
118	golden rain tree
119	flowering crabapple
121	Young's weeping birch
122	weeping copper beech
123	weeping white pine

Broad-leaved evergreens

110	rhododendrons
144	compact strawberry bush
145	California lilac
147	Oregon grape
148	Chinese heavenly bamboo

Conifer shrub

107	dwarf spreading English yew

Deciduous shrubs

124	summersweet
125	flowering quince
127	beauty bush
129	mock orange
130	doublefile viburnum
131	butterfly bush
133	burning bush
135	fothergilla
137	fragrant sumac
139	azalea exbury

Ground Covers

146	lavender
150	rosemary
152	bugleweed
153	kinnikinnick (bearberry)
154	purple-leaf winter creeper
155	sand strawberry
158	thyme

Grasses

164	dwarf blue fescue
166	blue oat grass
168	crimson fountain grass
169	Adam's needle

(In Appendix A, refer to grass type, not preceding number.)

Vine

159	grape

APPENDIX A
PLANT VARIETIES AND CHARACTERISTICS

CONIFERS: TREES

No.	Plant name	Form	Ht. in 10 yrs.	Spread in 10 yrs.	Rate of growth	Root system	Exposure	Soils	Soil type	Low water use	Remarks, uses	Plant zone
100	Leyland cypress (Chamaecyparis) + other varieties	Colum.	8-10'	8-10'	1-2'	shallow	sun, p.shade	avg.	AC		screen, mixed border, windbreak	6 to 10
101	Lodgepole pine/ shore pine/jack pine (Pinus)	Psque.	8-10'	4-5'	10-12"	varies	sun	avg. to poor	AC AK	x	picturesque accent, naturalized groups, large room divider	3 to 10
102	Scotch pine (Pinus)	Colum.	15-20'	6-8'	4-6"	varies	sun, p. shade	sandy, poor	AC AK	x	windbreak, privacy	4 to 9

PLANT VARIETIES AND CHARACTERISTICS-2

CONIFERS: SHRUBS

No.	Plant name	Form	Ht. in 10 yrs.	Spread in 10 yrs.	Rate of growth	Root system	Exposure	Soils	Soil type	Low water use	Remarks, uses	Plant zone
103	Skyrocket juniper (Juniperis scopulorum) + other varieties	Colum.	6-8'	3'	slow	avg.	sun	avg. to poor	AK AC	x	mixed border, accent sgl./grouped, screen, room divider	2 to 9
104	Andorra juniper (Juniperis)	Colum.	3'	5-6'	slow	avg.	sun	avg.	AK AC	x	groundcover, sea banks	4 to 9
105	Bar Harbor juniper (Juniperis)	low	12"	5-6'	slow	avg.	sun	avg.	AK AC	x	groundcover, sea banks, alpine	2 to 9
106	Swiss mt. pine (Pinus) compact form	globe, psque.	4-5'	3-4'	slow	deep	sun	avg.	AK AC	x	accent, borders/masses, enclose, windbreak	4 to 8
107	Dwarf spreading English yew (Taxus)	low, globe	4-6'	2-3'	1-2"	shallow	p. shade	avg.	AK AC		groundcover, base planting, accents	4 to 8
108	Hicks yew (Taxus)	column.	5-6'	2-3'	1-2"	shallow	p. shade	avg.	AK AC	x	hedge, background, accent, border, room divider	4 to 8

PLANT VARIETIES AND CHARACTERISTICS-3

BROAD-LEAVED EVERGREEN: TREES

No.	Plant name	Form	Ht. in 10 yrs.	Spread in 10 yrs.	Rate of growth	Root system	Flowers	Exposure	Soils	Soil type	Low water use	Remarks, uses	Plant zone
109	Cherry laurel or English laurel (Prunus)	clump	6-8'	4-5'	6-8"	shallow	white	all	avg.	all		screen, windbreak, border	6 to 8
110	Rhododendron [some varieties 1-4'; some 4-6']	globe, clump	8-10'	4-5'	6-8"	shallow, fibre	varies	sun, shade	avg./ rich	AC		accent, border/room divider, screen, woodland	4 to 9

PLANT VARIETIES AND CHARACTERISTICS-4

DECIDUOUS TREES
(large scale)

No.	Plant name	Form	Ht. in 10 yrs.	Spread in 10 yrs.	Rate of growth	Root system	Flowers	Exposure	Soils	Soil type	Low water use	Remarks, uses	Plant zone
111	Flowering ash (Fraxinus) + other varieties	globe	30'	20'	4-6"	shallow	white	sun/ p. shade	avg.	AK N AC		large scale, filtered shade	4 to 8
112	Thornless honey locust (Gleditzia) + other varieties	globe	14-16'	10-12'	2-3"	deep	white	sun	rich but drought tolerant	AK N		filtered shade, large scale, climate control	4 to 9
113	Sweet gum (Liquidamber)	colum.	14-16'	8-10'	2-3"	deep		sun	well-drained	AC AK	x	large scale, street tree, fall color	5 to 9
114	Oak (Quercus) several species	globe	12-14'	8-10'	2-3"	deep		sun	well-drained/ sandy	AC N AK	x	large scale, accent, shade, fall color	4 to 8

These trees are too large for a very small garden. Some would fit on 12,000 to 13,000 sq. ft. lot.

PLANT VARIETIES AND CHARACTERISTICS-5

DECIDUOUS TREES
(small scale)

No.	Plant name	Form	Ht. in 10 yrs.	Spread in 10 yrs.	Rate of growth	Root system	Flowers	Exposure	Soils	Soil type	Low water use	Remarks, uses	Plant zone
115	Serviceberry (Amelanchier) Eastern & Western species varieties	globe	12-15'	8-10'	1-2"	deep	white	sun to shade	well-drained/ avg.	AC N	x	accent, fall color, patio tree, woodland/ natural, mixed border	4 to 8
116	Lavalle hawthorne & Washington thorn (Crataegus)	globe	8-10'	4-5'	1-2"	deep	white	sun, p. shade	avg.	AK N AC	x	accent, barriers, mixed border, woodland, attract birds	3 to 9
117	Snowdrop tree (Styrax) varieties Pink Chines	psque., globe	8-10'	6-8'	4-6"	deep	white, pink	sun, p. shade	rich/ well-drained	AK		accent, small scale, shade	5 to 9
118	Golden rain tree (Koelreuteria)	globe, psque.	12-15'	8-10'	2-3"	deep	yellow	sun	avg. to poor	AK		shade for small area, mixed border	5 to 9

PLANT VARIETIES AND CHARACTERISTICS-6

DECIDUOUS TREES - continued (small scale)

No.	Plant name	Form	Ht. in 10 yrs.	Spread in 10 yrs.	Rate of growth	Root system	Flowers	Exposure	Soils	Soil type	Low water use	Remarks, uses	Plant zone
119	Flowering crab (many varieties) (Malus)	globe, weeping	12-14'	8-10'	1-2"	deep	mixed	sun	heavy	AK N AC		space dividers, mixed border, espaliered, disease-free	5 to 7
120	Pagoda tree (Sophora)	round	12-15'	6-8'	2-3"	shallow/ deep	white	sun	sandy	AK N AC	x	shade, mixed border	4 to 8

WEEPING TREES

No.	Plant name	Form	Ht. in 10 yrs.	Spread in 10 yrs.	Rate of growth	Root system	Flowers	Exposure	Soils	Soil type	Low water use	Remarks, uses	Plant zone
121	Young's weeping birch (Betula)	weeping	15-20'	8-10'	2-3'	shallow		sun, p. shade	avg.	AK N AC	x	accent, border, screen	4 to 9
122	Weeping copper beech (Fagus)	weeping	10-12'	5-6'	2-3"	avg.		sun	avg.	AK AC		accent, border, sculptural	4 to 7
123	Weeping white pine (Pinus)	weeping	7-8'	4-5'	1-2"	avg.		sun/ shade	avg.	AK AC	x	accent, border, banks	4 to 9

PLANT VARIETIES AND CHARACTERISTICS-7

DECIDUOUS SHRUBS (tall)

No.	Plant name	Form	Ht. in 10 yrs.	Spread in 10 yrs.	Rate of growth	Root system	Flowers	Exposure	Soils	Soil type	Low water use	Remarks, uses	Plant zone
124	Summersweet (Clethra)	clump	8-10'	5-6'	2-3"	avg.	white/pink	sun	avg.	AC AK N		accent, border, room divider	3 to 9
125	Flowering quince (Chaenomeles)	clump	8'	5-6'	3-6"	avg.	varied	sun	avg. to poor	AC AK N	x	backgd, border, espalier, spring flower	4 to 8
126	Red osier dogwood (Cornus)	clump	12-15'	6-8'	6-12"	avg.	white	sun, p. shade	avg. or moist/ wet	AK AC N		enclosing spaces, bogs/wet, winter interest, background	2 to 8
127	Beautybush (Kolkwitzia)	clump	10'	5-6"	6-8"	avg.	pink	sun, p.	avg. to shade	AK poor AC		screen, border, background	6 to 9

PLANT VARIETIES AND CHARACTERISTICS-8

DECIDUOUS SHRUBS (tall -- continued)

No.	Plant name	Form	Ht. in 10 yrs.	Spread in 10 yrs.	Rate of growth	Root system	Flowers	Exposure	Soils	Soil type	Low water use	Remarks, uses	Plant zone
128	Privet (Ligustrum)	clump	10-12'	4-5'	10-12"	avg., surface	white	sun, p. shade	avg.	AK AC N		hedge, screen, background	3 to 8
129	Mockorange (Philadelphus)	clump	8-10'	4-5'	6-12"	avg. to shallow	white fragrant	sun, p. shade	avg.	AK AC N		background accent border	5 to 8
130	Doublefile viburnum (Viburnum)	globe	8-10'	4-5'	8-10"	deep	white	sun	avg.	AK AC N		screen, border, accent, fall color, espalier	4 to 8

DECIDUOUS SHRUBS (medium)

No.	Plant name	Form	Ht. in 10 yrs.	Spread in 10 yrs.	Rate of growth	Root system	Flowers	Exposure	Soils	Soil type	Low water use	Remarks, uses	Plant zone
131	Butterfly bush (Buddleia)	clump	5-6'	4-5'	1-2"	deep	blue, white, purple	sun	avg. to poor	AK AC	x	border/ background, seascape, enclose, attracts birds	4 to 9

PLANT VARIETIES AND CHARACTERISTICS-9

DECIDUOUS SHRUBS (medium -- continued)

No.	Plant name	Form	Ht. in 10 yrs.	Spread in 10 yrs.	Rate of growth	Root system	Flowers	Exposure	Soils	Soil type	Low water use	Remarks, uses	Plant zone
132	Korean barberry (Berberis) (other species and varieties)	clump	6'	4'	3-4'	avg.	yellow	sun	avg.	AC AK N	x	border, fall color, screen	5 to 9
133	Compact burning bush (Euonymus)	globe	5-6'	3-4'	2-3"	comp.		sun	avg.	AK AC		mixed border, enclose, fall color	3 to 8
134	Forsythia (Forsythia) (several varieties)	globe	5-6'	5-6'	5-6"	deep	yellow	sun/p. shade	avg.	AK AC		mixed border, accent, enclose	3 to 8
135	F. monticola (Fothergilla)	globe	3-4'	3-4'	1-2"	deep	white	sun	avg.	AK AC		mixed border, accent, fall color	4 to 8
136	Oakleaf hydrangea (Hydrangea)	globe	3-4'	3-4'	1-2"	comp.	white	p. shade, shade	avg.	AK AC		accent/mass, color in fall, winter interest	6 to 9
137	Fragrant sumac (Rhus) + other species & varieties	psque.	3-5'	5-8'	2-3"	deep	yellow	sun	poor	AC AK	x	bank cover, fall color, meadows	5 to 9
138	Rugosa rose (Rosa) (other varieties)	psque.	4-5'	3-4'	1-2"	avg.	var.	sun	any	AK AC	x	border, sun/ meadows, wild garden, seaside	2 to 7

PLANT VARIETIES AND CHARACTERISTICS-10

DECIDUOUS SHRUBS (medium -- continued)

No.	Plant name	Form	Ht. in 10 yrs.	Spread in 10 yrs.	Rate of growth	Root system	Flowers	Exposure	Soils	Soil type	Low water use	Remarks, uses	Plant zone
139	Exbury hybids (Azalea)	globe	4-5'	3-4'	3-4"	comp.	var.	sun/p. shade	rich	AC		border, accent, woodland	5 to 9

DECIDUOUS SHRUBS (low)

No.	Plant name	Form	Ht. in 10 yrs.	Spread in 10 yrs.	Rate of growth	Root system	Flowers	Exposure	Soils	Soil type	Low water use	Remarks, uses	Plant zone
140	Clavey's dwarf honeysuckle (Lonicera)	low	3'	3'	1-2"	avg.	white	sun/p. shade	avg.	AK N AC	x	mixed border, foreground, groundcover, base planting	3 to 9
141	Cinquefoil (Potentilla) (hybrids)	low	2-4'	3'	1-2"	avg.	yellow, orange	sun	avg to poor	AK AC	x	mixed border, foreground, groundcover, base planting	3 to 9
142	S. bumalda (Spirea) (several varieties)	low	2-3'	2-3'	1-2"	shallow	pink	sun,	any	AC		base planting, border, groundcover	all
143	Common snowberry (Symphoricarpos)	low	2-3'	2-3'	1-2"	shallow	pink	sun, p, shade	avg.	AC AK	x	groundcover, woodland, seascape	all

PLANT VARIETIES AND CHARACTERISTICS-11

BROADLEAVED EVERGREEN SHRUBS

No.	Plant name	Form	Ht. in 10 yrs.	Spread in 10 yrs.	Rate of growth	Root system	Flowers	Exposure	Soils	Soil type	Low water use	Remarks, uses	Plant zone
144	Compact strawberry bush (Arbutus)	globe, psque.	5-6'	4-5'	2-3"	comp.	white	sun	avg.	AC		screen/ divider, border, foundation, accent	8 to 10
145	California lilac (Ceanothus) + other species & varieties	globe, psque.	6-8'	4-5'	2-3"	avg.	blue	sun	avg.	AC	x	screen, border, accent/masses	7 to 9
146	Lavender (Lavendula)	low	2-3'	2-3'	1-2"	shallow	lav.	sun	avg.	AC AK	x	screen/ divider, border, seashore, drought	5 to 8
147	Oregon holly grape (Mahonia) (other varieties and species)	colum., low	3-4'	2-3'	1-2"	shallow	yellow	sun to shade	avg.	AC AK	x	border, hedge, screen, seashore	6 to 10
148	Nandina domestica (Nandina)	colum., psque.	4-5'	2-3'	2-4"	shallow	white	sun, shade	avg.	AC AK		accent, mixed border, room divider	6 to 9
149	Firethorn (Pyracantha) (many varieties)	globe, psque.	4-5'	3-4'	1-2"	deep	white	sun, p. shade	avg.	AK N AC	x	screen, attracts birds, train on walls, border	5 to 10

PLANT VARIETIES AND CHARACTERISTICS-12

BROADLEAVED EVERGREEN SHRUBS -- continued

No.	Plant name	Form	Ht in 10 yrs.	Spread in 10 yrs.	Rate of growth	Root system	Flowers	Exposure	Soils	Soil type	Low water use	Remarks, uses	Plant zone
150	Rosemary (Rosemarinus)	low	4-5'	4-5'	1-2"	shallow	blue	sun	avg. to poor	AC N AK	x	groundcover, low masses, foreground, container, drought	7 to 9
151	California way myrtle (Myrica californica) + eastern specie	clump, globe	8-10'	5-6'	1-2'	shallow	white	sun	avg.	N AK	x	privacy border, salt-water plantings, background	8 to 10

GROUNDCOVERS

No.	Plant name	Form	Ht in 10 yrs.	Spread in 10 yrs.	Rate of growth	Root system	Flowers	Exposure	Soils	Soil type	Low water use	Remarks, uses	Plant zone
152	Bugleweed (Ajuga) (several varieties)	low	4-8"	36-42"	2-4"	shallow	blue	sun, p. shade	moist, avg.	AC AK		creeping perennial, between stones, banks	5 to 9
153	Kinnikinnick (Arctostaphylos)	low	18"	3-4"	1"	shallow	pink, white	sun	sandy	AK N	x	hot slopes, low maintenance, seaside	2 to 9
154	Purple leaf winter-creeper (Euonymus)	low	2"	4-5'	6-8"	avg.		sun	avg. to	AC AK N	x	banks, low maintenance	5 to 10

PLANT VARIETIES AND CHARACTERISTICS-13

GROUNDCOVERS -- continued

No.	Plant name	Form	Ht. in 10 yrs.	Spread in 10 yrs.	Rate of growth	Root system	Flowers	Exposure	Soils	Soil type	Low water use	Remarks, uses	Plant zone
155	Sand strawberry (Fragaria)	low	6-8"	6"	2-3"	shallow	white	sun	avg. to poor	AC AK	x	hot banks, trailside, seaside	6 to 10
156	Japanese spurge (Pachysandra)	low	8-10"	18-24"	6-8"	shallow	white	shade	avg.	AC AK		around house, woodland, lawn substitute	5 to 9
157	Stonecrop (Sedum) (several species and hybrids)	low	4"	8-10"	2"	shallow	varies	sun, shade	avg. to poor	AC AK	x	groundcover, between stepping stones, rockery	4 to 9
158	Creeping thyme (Thymus)	low	2"	4'	4-6"	shallow	white, lav.	sun, p. shade	avg. to poor	AC AK	x	sideyards, groundcover for low maintenance, woodland	5 to 10

VINES -- DECIDUOUS

No.	Plant name	Form	Ht. in 10 yrs.	Spread in 10 yrs.	Rate of growth	Root system	Flowers	Exposure	Soils	Soil type	Low water use	Remarks, uses	Plant zone
159	Grapes hybrid (Vitis)	climbing	6-8'	6-8'	2"	shallow	white	sun	avg.	N		wire screens, fences, walls, trellises	7 to 10

PLANT VARIETIES AND CHARACTERISTICS-14

VINES -- DECIDUOUS -- continued

No.	Plant name	Form	Ht in 10 yrs.	Spread in 10 yrs.	Rate of growth	Root system	Flowers	Exposure	Soils	Soil type	Low water use	Remarks, uses	Plant zone
160	Bittersweet (Celastrus)	train	10-20'	10-20'	fast	deep	yellow	sun	avg.	AK AC		strong growing, needs training	all
161	Chinese wisteria (Wisteria)	train	15-20'	15-20'	fast	deep	white, purple	sun	avg.	AK AC	x	will grow into trees, on pergolas & walls, trellis, rails, fences	3 to 9

VINES -- EVERGREEN

No.	Plant name	Form	Ht in 10 yrs.	Spread in 10 yrs.	Rate of growth	Root system	Flowers	Exposure	Soils	Soil type	Low water use	Remarks, uses	Plant zone
162	Silver morning glory (Argyreia)	climbing	fast	fast	4'-5'	shallow	pink	sun	dry	N		wire screens, fences, walls, trellises	10
163	Clematis armandi (Clematis) 2 yr.	climbing	15-20'	3'		shallow	white, pink	shade	avg.	AC N		wire screens, fences, walls, trellises	8 to 10
164	Golden pathos (Epipremnum) 2 yr.	climbing	20"-40"	20"-40"	2"-3"	shallow		shade	dry	N		wire screens, fences, walls, trellises	10
165	Poet's jasmine (Jasmine) 2 yr.	climbing	6-8"	20"-40"	2"-3"	shallow	white	sun	avg.	N		wire screens, fences, walls, trellises	7 to 10

PLANT VARIETIES AND CHARACTERISTICS-15

WETLAND--TREES

No.	Plant name	Form	Ht. in 10 yrs.	Spread in 10 yrs.	Rate of growth	Root system	Flowers	Exposure	Soils	Soil type	Low water use	Remarks, uses	Plant zone
166	Paper birch (Betula)	clump	20-30'	6-10'	2-3"	shallow			p. shade	moist, avg.	AC AK		groups at waterside, white trunk (accent), large space divider, attracts birds	2 to 6
167	White oak (Quercus)	globe	16-20'	12-15'	1-2"	varies			sun. p. shade	very moist	AC AK N		in water, groups, shade	1 to 3, 10

GRASSES

No.	Plant name	Form	Ht. in 10 yrs.	Spread in 10 yrs.	Rate of growth	Root system	Flowers	Exposure	Soils	Soil type	Low water use	Remarks, uses	Plant zone
168	Dwarf blue fescue (Festuca)	colum.	1-3'			dies back, renews each yr.	blue	sun	well-drained	AK N AC	x	edging, accent, contrast w/grays, seashore	4 to 8
169	Sheeps fescue (Festuca)	colum.	1'			dies back, renews each yr.		sun	avg. to poor	AC AK		drought resist-ant, naturalize, meadows, edging	4 to 8
170	Blue oat grass (Helictotrichon)	low	2'	2-3'				sun	avg.			edging	1
171	Eulalia grass (Miscanthus)	clump	6'	5-6'					moist to wet				5

170

PLANT VARIETIES AND CHARACTERISTICS-16

GRASSES continued

No.	Plant name	Form	Ht. in 10 yrs.	Spread in 10 yrs.	Rate of growth	Root system	Flowers	Exposure	Soils	Soil type	Low water use	Remarks, uses	Plant zone
172	Crimson fountain grass (Pennisetum)	clump	2-3'	3-4'					sun, p. shade	avg.	AK AC			8
173	Adams needle (Yucca)	clump	3-4'	3-4'					sun	avg. to dry	AK AC			8
174	Crested wheat grass Bearded couch	colum.	1'-3'						sun, p. shade	avg. to poor	AK N AC	x	drought resistant, naturalize in open & shady areas, seeded	3 to 8
175	Dwarf blue fescue (Festuca)	tufted	6"-12"			fine	green		sun	well-drained	AK N AC	x	edging, accent. contrast w/grays, groundcovers, seashore	4 to 8
176	Native yuccas Beargrass + other species	linear	3'-4'			heavy	white		sun	poor	AK N	x	accent, naturalize, rock garden	4 to 10
177	Pond sedge	mound	1'-2'			medium	green, white stripe		sun	moist	AK N		perennial border, rock garden, water garden, accent	5 to 9
178	Rye grass Barclay + other varieties	upright	8"-12"			medium	green		sun	avg. to poor	AK N AC	x	naturalize, erosion control, lawns	all

PLANT VARIETIES AND CHARACTERISTICS-17

GRASSES continued

No.	Plant name	Form	Ht. in 10 yrs.	Spread in 10 yrs.	Rate of growth	Root system	Flowers	Exposure	Soils	Soil type	Low water use	Remarks, uses	Plant zone
179	Sheeps fescue (Festuca)	tufted	1'					sun	avg. to poor	AC AK N	x	drought resistant, naturalize, meadows, edging	4 to 8
180	Side oats grama Chino grass seed	tufted upright	1'-3'			fine, shallow	lt. green	sun	clay loam sandy	AK N	x	naturalize, meadows, erosion control	3 to 10
181	St. Augustine - green Buffalo grass seed	mound	3"-12"			fine, shallow	med. green	sun	well-drained	AK N	x	lawns, naturalize, meadows, invasive/ prune	9 to 10
182	Bermuda grass seed	spreading	6"			medium, shallow	green	sun	avg. to poor	AK N AC	x	drought resistant, mat-forming/ erosion	8 to 10

PLANT VARIETIES ESPECIALLY FOR WARM CLIMATES
(names only)

Broad-leaved evergreen trees:
Strawberry tree (Arbutus)
Crape myrtle (Lagerstroemia) - many varieties
Fraser photinia (Photinia)
Evergreen oaks (Quercus) - several species
Oleander (Nerium)
Dwarf pomegranate (Punica)

Shrubs:
Wayleaf privet (Pittosporum)
Pineapple guava (Feijsa)
Persian lilac (Syringa)
Flowering pomegranate (Punica)
Shrubby senna (Cassia)
Creosote bush (Larrea)

Miscellaneous:
Aleppo pine (Pinus)
Rattan palm (Raphis)
Desert willow (Chilopsis)
Pinon pine (Pinus)
Live oak (Heritage - Quercus)
Arizona cypress (Cypressus)

APPENDIX B

DESIGNED SURFACES—HARD AND SOFT
Hard surfacing materials

Substance	Comment about use
concrete	most versatile substance, but difficult for do-it-yourselfer can be molded into various shapes and patterns, including use of brick, wood, or metal dividers or edgers (to prevent cracking) finish can be aggregate (gravel mixed with concrete) or broomed, i.e., made non-skid) takes color and can be shaped to suit individual taste
unit pavers	usually cast from concrete in various shapes (e.g., rectangle, hexagon, circle) used in entry courts, patios/terraces, walks, and driveways fit together snugly in various locations cost is twice that of poured concrete must have good underlying drainage (crushed rock and sand)
random pieces	brick, flagstone, broken concrete, tiles, quarried rock, washed round "river" rock are among the possibilities permits exercise of artistry in designing patterns—from very formal to highly imaginative spaces between pieces can be planted with groundcover
wood	most commonly used for decks, especially where complicated angles are involved treated lumber can be laid directly on ground if good drainage underneath surface can become slippery in rainy climate cost is three times that of poured concrete
asphalt	used for driveways, play paths cost slightly less than concrete
temporary	if soil is porous and climate is temperate, cement mixed with sandy soil establishes temporary hard surface

DESIGNED SURFACES—HARD AND SOFT - 2
Soft surfacing materials

sand   may be coarse or fine
                        works in decorative gardens

crushed rock   types include basalt (browns), granite (grays),
                            sandstones (sometimes greens or blues)
                        fine size for paths and patios
                        coarser sizes for driveways and roads
                        coarsest size (3 to 6") for rip-rap on banks
                            and for drainage

gravel   sizes range from fine (pea gravel) to coarse
                            (cobblestone—6 to 8")

mulch   possibilities include:
                            rock and crushed brick (small volcanic rock
                                pieces for paths and in plant beds)
                            "landscape blanket" (manufactured fabric)
                            bark (for oversize paths, woodland walkways)
                            sawdust (less expensive than bark but causes
                                nitrogen depletion in soils)
                            wood chips (usually pine, used in children's
                                play areas and informal walkways)
                            peat moss (not recommended because of
                                depletion of natural bogs in Canada and elsewhere)
                            compost (recycled leaves and branches)

wood   squares and rounds (not recommended in rainy
                            climates because they become slippery)

lawn   may be seeded or sodded (rolls of fully
                            grown grass laid over topsoil)
                        cost is high (for seeding, rolling,
                            watering, fertilizing, mowing and trimming)
                        certain native grasses and drought-resistant
                            grasses (e.g., fescues, rye grasses) need
                            little topsoil, fertilizer, or mowing

lawn   wild strawberry, periwinkle (vinca),
substitute   kinnikinnick, and flat-growing juniper used in large areas
                        thyme and sedum used in warmer climates
                        no croquet possible on these surfaces

APPENDIX C

CAN COMPUTER-AIDED DESIGN HELP?

Go into nearly any design office—building architect, landscape architect, or urban planner—and you will see computer screens alive with drawings, often in glowing color. The footprints of buildings, lot perimeters, circulation patterns, and plant masses all appear with striking clarity and accuracy.

Ask the people who prepare these plans for a living whether the computer is really needed for such work. They're likely to say, "You bet. Couldn't get my work done without it."

Does this conversion from pencil- and pen-drawing to computer-aided design (CAD) mean that even amateur or part-time designers must also use a computer equipped with a powerful design program? For the kinds of designing we have suggested in this book, probably not. However, for any younger person who is thinking about a career in some aspect of landscape design, the use of such a program is probably unavoidable. The technique is rapidly becoming widespread—even commonplace—and the advantages of speed and flexibility are undeniable.

It is not our intention here to explain in any detail how a computer design program works. That requires reading a sizeable instruction manual and a considerable amount of hands-on practice with a program, such as AutoCAD. But we do want to give an overview of how you might use this aid.

Let's say that you have made your preliminary plot plan. (See Chapter 4.) You've got the boundary lines drawn with approximately the correct angles and shapes. Measurements are done and written down. You've sketched locations of principal utilities, and you've measured all major plant masses (trees and shrubs) and drawn them in.

Sitting at the computer equipped with AutoCAD, you will be using both a keyboard and a rectangular piece of plastic, called a digitizing tablet, that is connected to the computer by a wire. You'll tape your drawing to the tablet and, with a mouse (a mouse-shaped device with illuminated cross-hairs and pushbuttons that activate commands), transfer the hand-made drawing to the computer screen.

The program allows you to create several layers for the drawing, each in a different color, if you wish, and you'll be able to see any combination of layers together whenever you want. For instance, the house footprint and the utility-line layers might be viewed together. Or you could have major trees on one layer and view them along with the house and boundary-line layers.

Every time you draw a line on the tablet with the commands available in the program, the computer meticulously calculates its length, location, and angle. When it comes time to show plant materials—both existing and planned—you do that either by employing the program's array of circles, squares, rectangles, and triangles, or you can use the sketch command to doodle or draw freehand.

In other words, virtually anything you might have tried to put on a piece of paper can be done at the computer. Among the major advantages of using this procedure are speed, accuracy, and flexibility. You are free to create as many site plans and planting designs as your imagination and ingenuity may suggest. You can change any of them quickly. You can have them in 3-D if 2-D seems too limiting. You can determine square footage even for irregularly shaped parts of the plan, so, when you're ready to calculate costs for materials (like pavers or irrigation pipes or topsoil or bushes), you have an extremely accurate basis for estimates.

Any designs that you've created on the computer screen can be printed on paper, too. Not all computer printers will handle such work, however, particularly when the desired size of paper exceeds the printer's capacity. For those cases, a plotter is required: a printer that works with pens filled with ink.

Professional landscape designers often exchange disks with building architects so that both are working from exactly the same measurements and shapes for a given project. They also invest considerable time, of course, in learning the intricacies of a CAD program. The electronic drawing file has essentially replaced drafting techniques of even recent times. Anyone who expects to be employed as a designer must learn to use CAD with ease and fluency.

Computer programs for landscape design available in 1994:

<u>Autocad for Windows</u> and <u>Autocad LT for Windows</u> (IBM-compatible)

<u>Landscape</u> (IBM-compatible & Macintosh)

<u>Generic CAD</u> (Macintosh)

APPENDIX D

NOTES ON PRUNING

The principle of pruning:

> Cutting back branches of trees and bushes
> with care and forethought preserves the pleasingly
> natural shape of the plant, both encouraging new
> growth and preventing the plant from overwhelming
> anything near it (e.g., house, garden area, path).

Steps in deciding how to prune:
1. Stand back and look at the basic shape or pattern (i.e., the alignment of branches) of the tree or shrub.
2. Keep this pattern in mind when beginning to prune so that the end result will retain that shape.
3. Use a tree saw, tree lopper, or pruning shears, depending upon the diameter of the branches.
4. Make all cuts on an angle, cutting at branch joints not at ends of branches.
5. Stand back after pruning about one-third of the plant to check retention of basic shape. If it is hard to tell where you pruned, you are probably doing it right.

Which plants to prune:
- deciduous plants that bloom in spring (e.g., beauty bush, forsythia, quince) pruned right after they flower (because next year's flowers are on the new wood)

- summer-flowering plants (e.g., hydrangea, butterfly bush) pruned in early spring

- broad-leaved evergreens and conifers tipped and pruned in early spring or summer in scale with landscape design

Which plants not to prune:
- tall-growing deciduous plants left to their own devices (if too large for a space, then moved to a more appropriate one)

APPENDIX E

QUESTIONS & ANSWERS ON USING NATIVE PLANTS

What is a native plant?

Every region of the country has its <u>native</u> plants, that is, plants that grow in a setting without human intervention. The soil, water, and temperature conditions they need are present, and the ecological balance achieved over hundreds or thousands of years sustains these conditions. Such plants are also called <u>indigenous</u>, sometimes with the further limitation of specific growing conditions within a region, such as, a slope or coast.

Native plants are different from <u>naturalized</u> and <u>exotic</u> (or <u>ornamental</u>) plants: the former have been introduced from another region and have adapted to conditions in the new environment; the latter can exist in a non-native region only with extra care and protection from typical environmental conditions for the region.

Why do landscape designers try to use native plants?

At one time, native plants may have seemed unappealing to landscape designers simply because they were so common. If the property owner and the designer were attempting to get an original or startling effect, they chose non-native plants.

That approach has often proven mistaken, based on such criteria as enduring visual interest, cost, and maintenance. Many landscape designers and property owners in all parts of the country now consciously choose to incorporate as many native plants as possible in their designs.

Here are some of the specific reasons:
1. Native plants, when viewed in their natural settings, have beauty—quite a different kind of beauty than we may achieve with "foreign" species and varieties.
2. When native plants are kept together in their natural communities, they thrive.
3. Plant communities attract birds, butterflies, and other animals to remind humans of our place in the supra-human scheme of things.
4. Incorporating native plants into a landscape design is likely to reduce the cost of executing that design.
5. Year-round maintenance of native plants (e.g., water, fertilizer, protection from intense heat or cold) is inevitably less than for non-natives.

How can one find out which plants are native to a region?

Taking walks to observe plants is the most direct means of finding out which are native. For the complete beginner to this kind of observation, however, a guidebook is necessary. Most public libraries and many bookstores have one or more reference books for plants, and usually such books include in their descriptions the native region of each plant.

Nurseries often feature plants native to the region. Many nursery people are very willing to point out these plants and to discuss their growing conditions. Before anyone makes a major purchase at a nursery, though, a preliminary visit to see native plants in their normal field conditions is highly desirable.

What are some of the ways native plants can fit into a landscape design?

- Taller trees and shrubs: for screening

- Low-growing bushes and vines: for groundcover

- Grasses: for soil retention on slopes

- Wetland plants: for restoring old—or creating new—
  watercourses and ponds

APPENDIX F

HINTS ON DRAINAGE PROBLEMS

Whenever a site is on a lowland—as along great river bottoms and near stream courses—drainage is obviously an important issue for both building contractors and landscape designers. Or if the soil is predominantly heavy—a "gumbo" texture—water will not drain through and will sometimes sit for days on the surface. A very high water table can produce a similar effect.

One obvious solution where runoff from buildings is heavy but surrounding soils are fairly porous is to slope the soil away from the buildings. A 2% slope is often cited as sufficient to carry away most runoff water so that it does not form puddles or seep into the foundation.

Planting beds can also be raised from 4" to 8" above the level of the rest of the site so that plants do not sit in water. In arranging such beds, however, one must avoid blocking the natural runoff routes if puddles or pools are not to result.

When the runoff problem is more serious and more nearly constant, a more ambitious solution may be necessary. The "French drain" is one of them. From the source of the largest amount of runoff water, a pipe (ranging from 1/2" to 4', depending on the amount of water to be handled) is buried in a sloping trench. The pipe extends to a sump or to a bog garden, where plants that like their "feet wet" take full advantage of the drainage. A path might run atop the pipe, with a fine-crushed-gravel surface and rocks and grasses along the sides, as suggested in the sketch below.

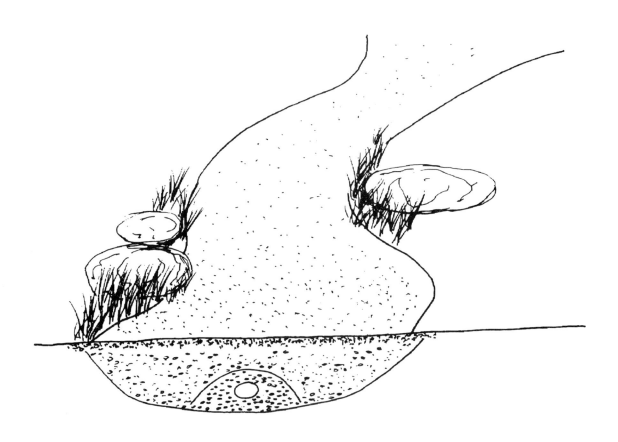

APPENDIX G

PRINTED REFERENCES & GARDEN-RELATED ORGANIZATIONS

The world abounds in printed reference materials on all aspects of plant materials and landscape design. Similarly, many organizations provide information of interest to garden designers. In many parts of the United States, larger colleges, universities, and county governments have cooperative extension divisions, which offer abundant printed information. Following are short lists of typical references that are readily available and not costly and of relevant organizations:

Books:
Gardening with Native Plants of the Pacific Northwest. Arthur Kruckeberg
Sunset Western Garden Book. Sunset Publishing Group. Several editions
Trees and Shrubs for Pacific Northwest Gardens. Marvin E. Black. Timber Press, 1990
Wildflower Handbook. Texas Monthly Press, Austin TX

Organizations:
American Association of Nurserymen (Washington D.C.)
American Horticultural Society (Alexandria VA)
Brooklyn Botanic Garden (Brooklyn NY)
Center for Plant Conservation (St.Louis MO)
Horticulture Dept., Cooperative Extension Service, Purdue University (West Lafayette IN)
U.S. National Arboretum (Washington D.C.)

APPENDIX H

SUGGESTIONS ON ARTIFICIAL GARDEN LIGHTING

A completed garden design may bring satisfaction during daylight hours. Must it be invisible and therefore less enjoyable at night? Not if the designer uses artificial lighting with skill.

Furthermore, the safety of people moving about the site may be a consideration. Properly placed lights can help assure that people will not fall on stairs or walkways.

Garden-lighting systems are readily available at relatively low cost, with installation well within the capability of most people. They operate at low voltage (12 v.), with a transformer at the exterior electrical receptacle. Wires supplying power to individual lights are best buried in a hand-dug trench 6" to 8" deep.

Common options for placing each light fixture are the following:

<u>uplighting</u> - a spotlight placed beneath a tree or vine accents shapes and textures

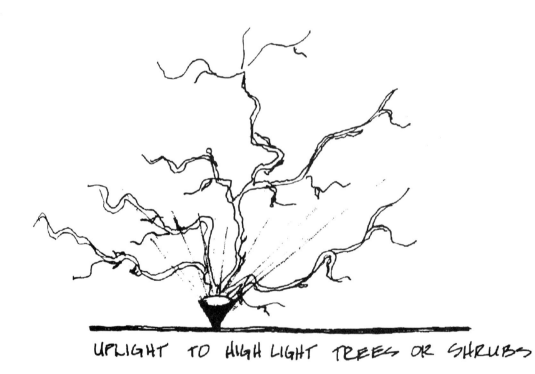

UPLIGHT TO HIGH LIGHT TREES OR SHRUBS

<u>highlighting</u> - a spotlight placed a few feet away from a tree
or bush that is next to a wall reveals its branching pattern

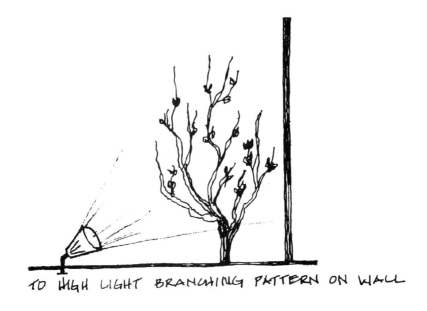

TO HIGH LIGHT BRANCHING PATTERN ON WALL

<u>downlighting</u> - a fixture that distributes light in a
wide arc marks turns in a walkway or other features deserving
notice for safety and/or aesthetic effect

PATHWAY LIGHT OR DOWN LIGHT ON FOLIAGE

An important consideration in deciding on the number and placement of outside lights is
subtlety. Too many lights and too much brightness can produce a garish effect, turning a home
into something resembling a commercial establishment.

APPENDIX I

SAMPLE PLANTING DESIGN FOR RURAL SITE

As a supplement and alternative to the planting design shown in Chapter 16 (Figure 16.6, p. 153), the following planting design is for a rural site—a pie-shaped lot. The owners of this site had these needs and desires:

- protection from cold winds

- privacy

- play space for children and adults

- private entry courtyard

- interesting features (e.g., pool, sculpture, boulders, meadow, wildflowers) visible from inside the house.

The owners also wanted to create a design that they could execute over a period of years because their budget did not allow quick and complete installation of all elements.

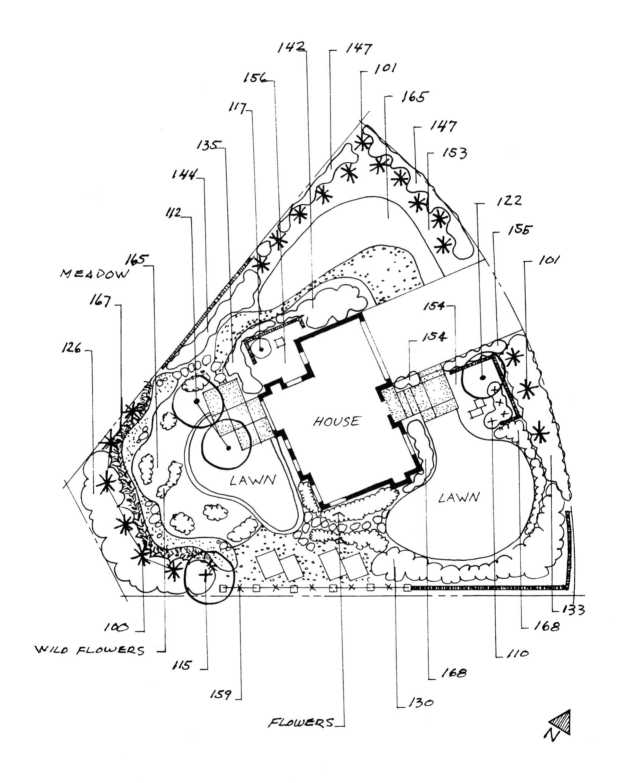

Planting Design for Rural Site

NAMES OF PLANTS SHOWN IN SAMPLE PLANTING DESIGN
FOR RURAL SITE

Trees

100	Leyland cypress
101	lodgepole pine
112	thornless honey locust
115	serviceberry
117	snowdrop tree
122	weeping copper beech

Deciduous shrubs

126	red osier dogwood
130	doublefile viburnum
133	compact burning bush
135	fothergilla
142	spirea bumalda

Broadleaved evergreens

110	rhododendron
144	compact strawberry bush
147	Oregon grape

Groundcovers

153	kinnikinnick
154	purple-leaf winter creeper
155	sand strawberry
156	Japanese spurge

Grasses

165	sheep's fescue
167	Eulalia grass
168	crimson fountain grass

(In Appendix A, refer to grass type, not
preceding number.)

Vine

159	grape

Index

NOTES AND DRAWINGS

NOTES AND DRAWINGS

NOTES AND DRAWINGS

NOTES AND DRAWINGS

NOTES AND DRAWINGS

NOTES AND DRAWINGS

NOTES AND DRAWINGS

NOTES AND DRAWINGS

Order Form

To order additional copies of:

Creating Good Landscape Design
A Guide for Non-Professionals

please send $17.95 plus $2.50 Shipping & Handling,
Washington residents please include 8.2% sales tax. Make check or money order payable to:

Peanut Butter Publishing
226 2nd Ave W.
Seattle, WA 98119
(206) 281-5965

If you prefer to use VISA or Mastercard, please fill in your card's number and expiration date.
Please circle appropriate card.

☐ ☐ ☐ ☐ ☐ ☐ ☐ ☐ ☐ ☐ ☐ ☐ ☐ ☐ ☐ ☐

Signature_____

exp. date_____
_____Copies @ $17.95 ea._____
$2.50 Shipping & Handling_____
Washington State residents add 8.2%_____
Total enclosed_____

Name_____
Address_____
City, State, Zip_____

Please list additional copies to be sent to other addresses on a separate sheet.